Walk On

MARNEY WILSON MATHERS

with

John Mathers

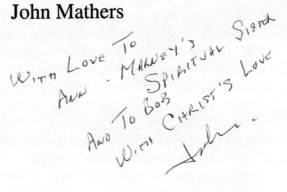

With Love To
Ann - Marney's
Spiritual Sister
And To Bob
With Christ's Love
John

CONTENTS

FOREWORD

This book was born out of the unique union of Marney and John Mathers. Marney was a prolific journal keeper. Her works stand more than two feet high. After her death, John began the task of sifting and sorting. He converted her words from prose into poetry; within, you will find a narrative of Marney's life and an expression of their enduring and joyful marriage of forty-four years. Where there were gaps, John wrote what she had expressed to him in their many conversations together. During her illness she gave John permission to share her journal as "he feels is helpful" thus extending her life's motto "to live for the glory of God and the good of many" beyond her earthly life. Marney died on October 25, 1998, after a two-year struggle with cancer.

Marney's Family

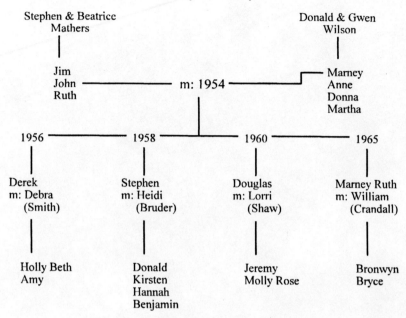

Stephen & Beatrice Mathers

Jim
John —————— m: 1954 —————— Marney
Ruth   Anne
                                       Donna
                                       Martha

Donald & Gwen Wilson

1956 —————— 1958 —————— 1960 —————— 1965

Derek
m: Debra
(Smith)

Holly Beth
Amy

Stephen
m: Heidi
(Bruder)

Donald
Kirsten
Hannah
Benjamin

Douglas
m: Lorri
(Shaw)

Jeremy
Molly Rose

Marney Ruth
m: William
(Crandall)

Bronwyn
Bryce

7

PROLOGUE

It so happened that Marney was born
   minutes before midnight on December 24th,
   minutes before Christ's birthday.
It also so happened that Marney remained
   just that close to Jesus
   throughout her life.

Marney was born insightful, intuitive and bold,
   leading those who must ponder to a decision
   and those of a shyer disposition
      aghast at her swift judgments and conclusions,
      as well they might be, because at times
         her insightfulness was flawed,
         her intuition failed, and
         her boldness hurt.
Most of the time, however, she used these gifts
   lovingly and well.
Her life's motto, a paraphrase of scripture,
   was "to live for the glory of God
      and the good of many."
Marney was raised in a conservative Christian family
   and was baptized as a believer at age three,
   an event she remembered in detail
      and cherished all her life.
During her life she was
   an interior designer and decorator,
   store owner and manager,
   sexual dysfunction therapist,
   Asian refugee advisor and placement coordinator,
   Red Cross volunteer in Okinawa,
   church leader for women and youth,
   wife, lover and mother,
      and always an artist, gardener and bird lover.

9

All this is but background to her
    deep, soul-penetrating,
    mystical Christian faith.
Before daily Christian journaling was popular
    Marney journaled, wrote and prayed.
She wrote almost daily
    and prayed as a style of living.
She knew Oswald Chambers'
    My Utmost For His Highest almost by heart
    and found new insights and new truths
    to guide her daily walk.

This then is the Marney who had cancer surgery at age sixty-five,
    apparently successful but only apparently,
    for eighteen months later a recurrence was found.
She knew she was dying;
    she died five days less than five months
    from the finding of her unexpected cancer return.
But, how did she die?
    When she awoke from her surgery,
    I was the one who told her of the recurrence.
        Her immediate reply was a very quiet "Oh no."
    During her time sick and in bed she often said
        "I don't mind dying, I just don't like the process."
        Even with increasing pain, complaints were few.
        She asked for pillows and support
            to make her comfortable.
She did not complain, whine or ask "Why me?"
She was not angry at God.
She planned to use her dying
    "For the glory of God and the good of many."
Her stated up front and specific goal
    was to model "Christian dying" to her family
    especially to her ten grandchildren
    so they would learn and come to know
    that death was tolerable, acceptable,
    and even, toward the end,

to be anticipated with joy by Christians.
Jesus said "Suffer the little children to come unto me."
    Marney invited, insisted and maybe even forced
    her grandchildren and their friends
        to climb up on her bed to play, to hug, to talk,
        to cuddle and even sleep with their Nana.
When Marney "Nana" died, the children were sad,
    but they were neither frightened nor afraid,
    for their Nana had taught them
        that the love of God, not only in this world
        but also in the next, neither fails nor disappoints
        for God's love is "new every morning."
So she and the children prayed and loved,
    spending God's time together.
How then did she treat grownups?
    In exactly the same way!
Adults, too, were required to climb up on her bed
    to commune with God and Marney,
    some to rest, hug and sleep,
    others to be challenged within their faith.
Many who visited left feeling blessed, uplifted
    and strengthened in their faith.
Eight weeks before she died Marney traveled
    850 miles to visit with and say goodbye
    to her mother, who spent a whole afternoon
    (you guessed it) lying in bed with her daughter
    praying, hugging, sleeping, loving,
    and saying goodbye to this world.
Her trip sapped her physical strength
    but gave comfort and completion to her soul.
Even in her last weeks, this was not a somber time,
    although surely a sad reason
    for being together.
We played games, we read;
    the kids watched cartoons and videos;
    we appreciated art and beauty;
    we prayed, we sang, we lived!

Death for Marney was triumphant
and now she lives triumphantly with Jesus!

John Mathers
March 1999

Walking Day by Day

April 7, 1985   Easter Sunday

Easter is a time of new beginning for me.
Buds are bursting on the trees.
Birds are singing in the early morning.
The sun is up before I am.

A time of new life
      both in nature and in my spirit:
      a renewal time in the Lord Jesus Christ
            a significant time in the church year
                  as we remember our Lord's resurrection.

Come let us pick up the armor of God
      which he has given us.
Let us be ready with new strength
      to follow Jesus Christ:
            our teacher
            our guide
            our Savior.

Undated, 1985

When some grievous thing happens in my life,
      I want to be alone with God and the Holy Spirit.
I may become rude (or abrupt) with others
      who want to pry me open at those times.

Our dog sometimes gets a thorn
      in his lovely big paw.
He goes to a corner of the house
      where there is no people traffic
      and there he works on getting the thorn out.
Sometimes I kneel beside him
      and we work together to remove the thorn.

15

I am like our dog.
When the thorns of life hurt
    I go to a quiet place
    and try to hide.
It may take hours,
    days,
    or weeks...
    but God is there,
    helping me to pull the thorn out.

July 27, 1985

"Come with me by yourselves
    to a quiet place
    and get some rest,"
        Jesus invited his apostles in Mark 6:31.

And God says to me,
    "Let the past pass away from you.
        Rest quietly in me.
        Let me fill you anew with my Holy Spirit.
    Be still now and know that I am God.
    I am he who is the physician.
        I know your pain.
        I know pain of the mind.
        I know physical pain.
        I know pain of the soul.
    Rest now in me.
    You will gain new strength
        to go on in my ministries
        but, for now, be still
        and rest in me.
    Let the world go on.
    Just be still
        and let my love flow through you
        for you will need it later.

Don't worry about houses
    or what you will wear
    or where John will work.
Be still and know that I am God.
I am with you always.
Rest, now, in me."

July 30, 1985

One of my sons
    brought me coffee and fruit bread.
        We talked.
I have been angry with him.
I asked forgiveness.
    He told me of the "black blob" in his life
        and the "white pearl."

Are not all our lives
    full of black blobs?
The great thing is that God,
    through Christ,
    washes clean the blobs.

I bless you, Lord,
    and thank you
that the black blobs in all our lives
    are cleared through Jesus Christ,
        your son,
replaced by a gift of great value,
    a white pearl:
        your sacrifice for us.

Undated, 1985

Sometimes I write letters
    to people I feel led to write to.
When people say, "Thank you for your letter.
It said just what I needed to hear,"
    I am surprised
    because I've forgotten what I wrote to them.
At times I receive similar letters
    which meet my needs:
the Holy Spirit,
    powerful and mysterious,
    at work.

January 7, 1986

As the sun breaks forth from the darkness,
    its rays hit the waters of Lake Superior
    and the shoreline,
        covered in snow,
        becomes golden pink.
The mist starts to rise and disappear.
It certainly is a day to rejoice.

Rejoice, and again I say rejoice!
We have our hope
    our certainty
    in and through our Savior, Jesus Christ.
Arise and serve the Lord with gladness
    for this is the day that the Lord has made.
Let us rejoice and be glad in it.

And now,
    on to the new adventures
    this day will bring.
Thank you, God.

May 30, 1986

The sight of a scarlet tanager,
    what a gift.
Holding a hummingbird in my hands,
    what a gift.

There is so much good in the natural world
    all nature sings,
    lives for the glory of God.
Pity the men and women
    who have turned their backs to the beauty of
    the scruffy old jay,
    the delicate breath of the hummingbird,
    red geraniums on a deck,
    the white jasmine that sends
        its scent into the air,
    the gull as it soars,
        letting wind currents carry it,
    the deep blue of the lake.

All live to the glory of God.
God, who is in this world.
God who, through Jesus Christ, is revealed to men and women,
    and to all human beings.

July 7, 1986

We have just passed the first day of summer.
We are receiving almost eighteen hours of light a day.
    The birds and animals are making the most of the light hours.
    The days are warm.
    It is a beautiful time of the year.

As I write this the goldfinches are coming to the feeder.
The sun plays on their yellow bodies.

They are golden in its light.

The plants are thriving.
Even the houseplants reach out to the light and warmth.

Light and heat are so important.
Without sun, there would be no world,
    just a frozen mass.

Is it not so with mankind?
If there is no light and heat in a man or woman,
    is not he or she a frozen mass to God?

As we come to know Christ, we thaw
    until there is no frost within us,
    until we are warm with the light of God
        and, sometimes, hot with the fire of the Holy Spirit.
Those who come near to us are drawn to the heat
    may even catch fire.

July 14, 1986

Lord, sometimes valleys are very pleasant
    the darkness restful,
    the food delicious.

I see your light starting up the mountainside
    and I hesitate,
    thinking of staying in the valley
    with friends who are there.

But I hear you call,
    "Come on, there is more to do.
    You are not finished yet, Marney."

I answer,
    "But Lord, how come they
    don't have to go any farther?"

And I hear you answer,
    "Their race is not your race of salvation.
    You will see them later,
        when your race is finished.
    Climb on, run when you can,
        walk when you need to.
    Crawl when it is necessary.
    I am before you."

Just so is the race of salvation I run
    with Jesus, my Lord, as the torch
    to lighten and brighten my way.

January 22, 1987

If I am not being continually
    refreshed in God's Spirit
    I become stale and have no love to give,
    no refreshing love.
Often I feel lonely, lost and unloved but,
    as I renew my spirit in him once,
    or many times, a day
    I am freshened and refreshed in my soul.
So I must jealously guard my relationship
    with God, Jesus and Spirit
    that I may remain
    one with them.

What a gift!

January 29, 1987

Lord,
    you ask us to love
    but your requirements to truly love
    overwhelm me:
"If I speak with the tongues of men and of angels,
    but do not have love,
    I have become a noisy gong or a clanging cymbal.
And if I have the gift of prophecy,
    and know all mysteries and all knowledge;
    and if I have all faith,
    so as to remove mountains,
    but do not have love,
    I am nothing.
And if I give all my possessions to feed the poor,
    and if I deliver my body to be burned,
    but do not have love,
    it profits me nothing.
Love is patient,
    love is kind,
    and is not jealous;
    love does not brag
    and is not arrogant,
    does not act unbecomingly;
    it does not seek its own,
    is not provoked,
    does not take into account a wrong suffered,
    does not rejoice in unrighteousness,
    but rejoices with the truth;
    bears all things,
    believes all things,
    hopes all things,
    endures all things.
Love never fails," Paul tells us in 1 Corinthians 13:1-8.

Father, how dare I ask for this love of yours,

for surely I blunder.
Lord, heal my mistakes,
    forgive my blundering ugliness,
    forgive me when, to ease my own frustration,
    I am impatient
    and seek my own way.

Love endures all things.
Because that can hurt,
    I seek to endure little.
My love is selfish,
    "seeks its own."
Love bears,
    hopes,
    believes,
    all, for me, a very big load.
Love never fails.
My love is always imperfect and often fails.

Lord, no matter how big your love is,
    no matter how much I fail,
    I am willing to try
    if you will teach me.
I know that in your love
    you will treat me gently.
Please be with me
    and if I should run back to you frightened
    enclose me in your bosom
    until I am ready
    to venture forth again.
Help me Father,
    through Jesus and his Spirit,
    to learn to love your way.
If you give me other gifts
    along the way,
    let me remember they come
    as tokens of your love.

Help me to go your way.
Hold my hand and guide me
    to a purer love.
Help me to follow as you lead
    enjoying your company always
    through Jesus Christ, your son.

February 2, 1987   Maui

This morning I feel "pushed" to walk the beach
    while John jogs on ahead.
I'm missing my usual time with God
    but this morning God speaks to me
    through the waves.

The footprints of people ahead of me
    are washed out by the next wave,
    as God's cleansing power
    through Jesus Christ,
    washes us.

The strength of the waves
    raises questions:
    Who can stop them?
    Who can harness their power?
Some are of great strength.
Some come as quietly and gently
    as the brush of a feather.
God is like this in my life:
    sometimes so strong,
    sometimes gentle as a feather.
His waves both knock me over
    and help me stand again,
    teaching me
    as I grow in his understanding and love.

The meeting of the outgoing waves
and the incoming waves
is one of thunderous power,
sending spray high into the air,
washing far onto the beach,
sweeping away debris from the sand,
even as I welcome God's cleansing waves
washing through me,
cleansing me,
making me fit to be one with his plans.

When the waves crest
and spray into the air,
they catch the early morning sunlight
and create tiny rainbows!
Promises from God.
God in the beauty,
a tremendous gift
from his hand,
a powerful, promising gift
a rainbow at the end of my walk.
Who "pushed" me to walk the beach?

April 4, 1987

My God is in a rainbow's iridescent colors,
in violets,
roses,
lilies of the field,
in quiet, shady spots
beside babbling brooks,
in thunderstorms,
volcanoes erupting,
and tidal waves.
My God is in the beauty of a newborn baby
held to a mother's breast,

25

and in the smell of human milk.
My God is in the cancer-riddled body
of a beloved friend
being released through death into new life.
My God is in patient, loving parents.
My God lives within me,
instructing me in love.
My God lives beyond the comprehension
of man or woman.
My God is found everywhere.
I am his creation.
I live for his glory.

April 24, 1987

I must constantly be in touch with God.
When I don't have time for him,
beware!
God is the one who does the growing part;
he builds,
and creates.
My part may be planting
or watering,
but to do even that
I must keep in touch with God
through daily
worship of him,
the one and only.

I must beware of any work *for* God
which enables me to evade concentration on him.
I must never worship my own work
(how very often this happens).
I must be constantly in touch with the Father,
do all things for and to the glory of him;
otherwise, the work will be stopped.

Help me, Father,
    to keep you at the center.
It is your work, not mine.
Keep me from being self-centered,
    wishing I could be the one
    to see the work finished.

May 1987

Jesus never mentioned
    unanswered prayer.
He had a boundless certainty
    that prayer is always answered.

May 1, 1987

Trusting is very difficult for me,
    especially when I believe:
        "I must be in charge of my own life."
        "I'll do it my way."
        "My problems are my problems.
            I'll solve them myself."
If I am a child of God, his child,
    he cares about all my problems,
    from the smallest to the biggest.
Even knowing that,
    I still find it difficult
    to trust him completely.
It is hard to hand him the reins!
It is like going out on a very high diving board
    or a high swinging bridge made of rope.
Halfway there, trusting,
    I look down at the water
    or deep ravine below
    and I want to turn back.

If I do, I will have to
    start over again
    or give up.

Trust is when I dive off the board
    or continue across the unsteady bridge.

June 15, 1987

It was in pure humbleness that Jesus
    took the towel and the basin
    and washed his disciples' feet.
Am I too proud to wash (so to speak)
    my neighbors' feet?
When I get rebuffed
    do I realize that true humility
    does not feel rebuff
    (or does it)?
True humility led to a cross.

Can I follow?
Do I have humility?
Am I able to wash feet?

June 20, 1987

Jesus Christ is the one I follow.
He has given me
    my map for this world.
If I become like him in my daily walk
    there is no need to talk nor push
    conversion on the people I meet.
It is a natural outcome
    of my obedience to him
    that people are drawn to him.

28

I am drawn closer to Christ
    when I see a group of women
    working selflessly with refugees.
The love they give
    is drawn from the love of Christ,
    from the worship of the Father,
    from the Eucharist
        communion
        the Lord's Supper.
Do they preach? No.
But the love of Christ
    shines as they
    tend his sheep.
My faith deepens
    from their example.

Thank you God.

August 4, 1987

Jesus chose twelve men,
    mainly uneducated fishermen.
God, through Jesus, has chosen us.
We can't be used by him
    unless we,
    in our own eyes,
    are worthless
    and empty of bias.
It is not a question
    of our being qualified
    to serve him
    but
    a question
    of our poverty.
It is not a question
    of what we bring to God

but of what God puts into us.
The only thing that matters
    is that we are taken up
    by our compelling God
    and made his comrades
    "Because the foolishness of God
        is wiser than men,
        and the weakness of God
        is stronger than men."
           (1 Corinthians 1:25)

August 25, 1987

Jesus said,
    "Greater love has no one than this,
    that he lay down his life for his friends."
        (John 15:13)

John's two aunts were seventeen years apart in age,
    but extremely close throughout life.
As the years went by
    and Aunt G approached ninety,
    Aunt J provided the physical
    and emotional support
    her sister needed.
Only after Aunt G died
    did she go to her doctor
    to check on her bladder
    which had been bleeding
    for years.
Aunt J intuitively knew
    the bleeding indicated
    cancer was present,
    but
    she gave the time
    proper treatment

would have taken
    to her sister's care.
She died of bladder cancer
    shortly after her sister's death.
Greater love...

September 7, 1987

While in Okinawa I found
    the "true meaning" of Christianity.
If I told a Japanese person
    I was a Christian,
    the response was often,
    "I know you are from the United States.
    Christian means Hollywood and movies."
They thought Christianity
    was synonymous
    with western culture.
But if I said,
    "I am a follower of Jesus Christ,"
    they understood me to mean
    I follow Christ's way for me.

January 1, 1988

Happy New Year!
And yet I have to wonder,
    what will this year bring?
    (Another new grandchild!)

Being a child of God,
    I know that he is with me.
He is for me and for our family.
Our welfare is in his hands.

It is not what I can do
    but what the king, God,
    can do through me.

Am I willing to let him work through me?
Is my trust in God great enough?

I agree with Paul's words in Philippians 1:20-21:
    "...my eager desire and hope being
        that I may never feel ashamed,
        but that now as ever
        I may do honour to Christ
        in my own person by fearless courage.
    Whether that means life or death, no matter!
    As life means Christ to me, so death means gain." (Moffatt)

Would that I may grow deeper in him:
    that I may turn over more of myself to the Lord,
    that I may learn more of his presence
    and that others might see him in me,
        his beauty,
        his love,
        his presence,
        his hope.
I don't know how that will work out
    or how I can show his love.
Maybe the better question is
    how will he show his love
    through me?

I must ask him to put Marney aside
    and work through me.

February 26, 1988

How open am I to his presence?
Am I, moment by moment, open to him?
He is always here
    but am I?

Marriage is a good example of this.
We, as husband and wife,
    must be open for one another's needs.

This is hard in a marriage relationship coming,
    as we do,
    from different backgrounds and cultures.
        She from a female
        and he from a male
            point of view,
                often she more a giver
                    than he.
But God is a giver.
Jesus Christ is a giver.
So this, I believe:
    males and females must learn
    to be more giving
        more submissive to each other
    and ultimately more submissive to God.

As we learn to do this
    we will become completely filled with his Holy Spirit
    and not with our own will.
We will become one with him.
And after intercourse,
    when a husband and wife come closer,
    there is tenderness.
Love flows through them
    to each other and to their children
    and it is easier to communicate love to others.

It is the same sort of thing with God.
As I have tender daily times with him,
    so our relationship grows.
His beauty comes to me.
His joy comes to me.
His love flows through me.
    I become his.

December 20, 1988

Christian radio stations have a lot of *sentimental stuff*:
    "How the baby looks,"
    "Eyes like stars"
        and so on!
I have to turn it off.

Granted, this is a season
    of special remembrance of Jesus' birth.
But gooey sentiment turns me off.
Praise and adoration are needed.
Glorify God,
    that he came to the men and women
    of this world to live as our perfect example,
        to show us what God himself is like,
        and to die and be resurrected for our salvation.

Christmas was originally held
    at the time of a pagan holiday.
Now, being on the commercial side of things
    with my store,
    I have to wonder if we are not still very pagan!
It is the time of year to make a quick dollar.
I see little of *Christ* in the *mass*.
Even Christian organizations
    hound people for money.
Where can we find Jesus today?

Where do we find Jesus today?
Do I know where to find him for myself?
I see cold plastic figures
    standing in creches
    on people's lawns,
    in store windows,
    and in church yards.
What do they mean?
What is their message?
Do people find Jesus there?
Only God knows.

Where is Jesus today?
To find Jesus,
    I must find his cross.
Even as we celebrate his birth,
    the cross needs to be central in our faith.
He died for the sins of all who have lived,
    who are even now alive
    with him.

What does the cross really mean?
I cannot grasp the full meaning of it.
I won't until I am with him.

Santa Claus is fun,
    but not central to Christmas.
Parties are fun,
    but not central to Christmas.
Central to Christmas
    is the praise and adoration of God
    for the gift of his Son.
Only then can Santa
    and parties
    and fun
    meaningfully add to the celebration of Christmas.

December 27, 1988

Yesterday was the ugliest day
    I have ever seen
        at the store;
    people bringing back gifts,
    trying to get the best deal at all costs.
By the end of it
    I wanted to throw up.

Jesus was only one day old
    and already forgotten.

January 11, 1989

If we insist on carrying our own cross
    we get so burdened down we cannot *follow* him.
If we let him take our cross
    our burden is light
    and we *skip along*
    following him with *a light load.*

O, why do I not learn this?
    I keep taking it back.

Matthew says, "And as they were coming out,
    they found a man of Cyrene named Simon,
    whom they pressed into service to bear his cross."
        (27:32)

Simon was in the right spot at the right time
    when someone was needed to serve Jesus.

Am I in the right spot for him to use me?
O that I am, daily as I turn to him.
I try to keep myself in his presence

(He is always in our presence.
We are the ones who turn our backs on him.)
Then I will be in the right spot
    at the right time
    to share a smile,
    a word of encouragement,
    to love with joy,
    to lighten someone's load
    and carry their cross a little way.

O Lord, make me a blessing.
Let your light shine through me.
Let your love shine through me
    to those I meet every day,
    wherever I am.
Let me be like Simon,
    a true servant,
    ready to serve you.

January 29, 1989

What manner of spirit am I?
I really don't know.
I think I do,
    but then I don't.
It would seem I am
    on the fringe of knowing.
It is something far greater than I (or we)
    can comprehend.
I think I almost have it,
    but then I don't!
I want to be right about it,
    but when I go to explain
    what manner of spirit I am
    or come from,
    I lose it!

January 13, 1989

Mostly, the times I spend alone with God
    are precious,
        but some are not so precious
        for I am shown myself.
How ignorant I am
    about myself.
Sometimes I have to ask,
    "Who am I?"

There is a lot I don't like,
    revealed
    as God peels the layers
    that have protected
    the inner me.
Sometimes it's not so bad,
    like the petals of a rose.
At other times,
    more like an onion.
God peels me slowly
    until, finally,
    we get to the nooks and crannies
    of my soul.
Unpleasant things are found there,
    things I must commit to his care,
    things that change only with my
        increasing daily dependence on Jesus
        as he works in me.

February 18, 1989

Sins.

It is not the big sins,
    murder and theft, that are my downfall.

It is, for me,
 the way I think,
 the opportunities I miss to serve,
 my preoccupation with self-interest.

It is in not glorifying God at all times.
My mind wanders to other things
 when I should keep my mind
 in his presence.
Practicing the presence of God
 in my life
 is very hard.

"What does the Lord your God require from you,
 but to fear the Lord your God,
 to walk in all His ways and love Him,
 and to serve the Lord your God
 with all your heart and with all your soul,
 and to keep the Lord's commandments and His statutes
 which I am commanding you today for your good?
Behold,
  to the Lord your God
  belong heaven and the highest heavens,
  the earth and all that is in it.
You shall fear the Lord your God;
  you shall serve Him and cling to Him,
  and you shall swear by His name."
   (Deuteronomy 10:12-14, 20)

By responding to this challenge
 I am practicing the presence of God.

March 14, 1989   Good Friday

"He must increase, but I must decrease,"
　　says John (3:30).

This is Good Friday,
　　the day our Lord Jesus died on the cross for us.

How long ago?
　　2000 and more years ago.

As I think upon that gift,
　　Jesus says to me:

"I was there at the beginning of the world
I was there in the garden.
I was there with the Father
　　when he led them through the Red Sea.
I was there when they lived in the desert.
I was there when they chose Saul to be king.
I was there with David
　　down through all the generations.
I was there.

"Then I was born as a baby in a lowly manger.
I came to them.
They rejected me.
They put me to death.
They were blind and could not see
　　that the Father and I are one.
I died for my own
　　at their hands."

God, the Father,
　　God, the Son,
　　and God, the Holy Spirit,
　　　　are one.

March 29, 1989

If you are avoiding the call of religious pressure
    and looking instead to Jesus,
      setting your heart on what he wants for you,
      you will be called impractical and dreamy.

Beware of those who would hinder your vision
    even if they appear to be the finest saints
    who ever walked this earth.
Center your life on Jesus
    and he will lead you through daily burdens.

April 20, 1989

God does things people expect least.
Our judgments are flawed
    and self-centered.
God will take the very things
    which have no value to us
    and place the highest value on them.

"That which is highly esteemed among men
    is detestable in the sight of God," says Luke (16:15).

April 23, 1989

Lord, I am tired.
This morning I am even tired of people
    and I am one of them.
We are so small in our thinking.
We try to limit your power,
    to conform with our limited knowledge.
Sometimes when I talk about
    your presence within me people say,

"That's not good theology."
It seems there are rules for theology.
People determine theology.
The church determines theology.
Ancient patriarchs determine theology,
    keep theology inside the church.
Rules, rules, rules.
Not yours, my God
    but theirs about you.

Sometimes I laugh.
Sometimes (most of the time) I cry.

May 18, 1989

"Look at the birds of the air,
    that they do not sow,
    neither do they reap,
    nor gather into barns,
    and yet your heavenly Father feeds them.
Are you not worth much more than they?
Observe how the lilies of the field grow;
    they do not toil nor do they spin,"
    Jesus exults in Matthew 6:26, 28.

More and more I am finding rest and peace.
I do not have to justify my actions to people.
I do not have to prove anything to them.
The only one who has to know is my Father, God.

People and their opinions will come and go.
The only one who remembers and cares is God.
Within a few years after my death
    people will have forgotten,
    but God,
        my Father,

who knows and loves me
and who is my judge,
will know and will remember.

So, for whom do I live?
I live for the glory of God
   just as the lilies do.

Only the Father knows.
Only the Father remembers.

I live for this moment.
I live for him.
I am to fill myself with his peace.
I am to empty myself of *self*
I am to become as a child to her mother,
   completely dependent.
When I do this,
   I am at peace,
   a peace unknown to the world.
I don't have to build myself up
   to prove my importance.
I am important to God.

The people who influence me most
   are not those who buttonhole me with talk
   but those who live their lives
      shining like the stars in the heavens
      or blooming like the lilies of the field,
   perfectly,
   simply,
   unaffectedly,
   in God's will.

Those are the lives that mold me!

June 5, 1989

Today, I grieve for China.
The people used their voices
    against the government
    only to be killed
    in Tiananmen Square
    —so peaceful when we were there.

Hundreds have been killed;
    students demonstrating against tyranny
    for freedom.

O Lord, my God,
    be with all peoples there
    (especially your people who love you).

Let them feel your presence
    in a mighty way.
Lord, send your angels to comfort them.
For freedom, they have given their lives:
    freedom of speech
    freedom of travel
    freedom of worship
    freedom of enterprise
    freedom from tyranny

The Lord is my helper.
The Lord is their helper.

June 14, 1989

There is a great parallel between a husband and wife
    and our relationship with God the Father,
        Son and
        Holy Spirit.

Both loving relationships
    are beautiful and holy.
In both we can rest
    in the security
    of perfect love.

In a human marriage love builds through years
    and it is the same in union with the triune God.
What is so very sad about marriages that break up
    is that sexual discord is often the reason.
The couple does not build their sensuality
    into a beautiful relationship of oneness,
    with each other,
    and with the Son,
        Father God, and
        Holy Spirit.
Marriages on earth are holy,
    but today they are like doormats to people.
They wear out from roughness
    and a new one is needed.
They are not treated as holy,
    beautiful creations,
    never completed
    but constantly worked on.

It is the same
    with our union with Christ.
We must remain in his love
    savoring his sweetness and love always.

July 12, 1989

I see in each Christian denomination
    aspects of the
    total personality of Jesus Christ.
Perhaps this is why

I find it hard to give myself
to only one denomination.
I live for the corporate Body of Christ.
I find him in this place
and that place.
I find him here;
I find him there.

When a denomination
or a church
begins to look inward,
after its own interests,
its own creeds
its own purposes,
the personality of Christ
dims in that place.

August 13, 1989

O Lord Jesus,
I feel like a stranger in and where I live.
I feel I don't own anything.
I am lonely.
I know my home is not here.
I long to come home to you.
I get so tired of people.
I see such pain
and I don't understand it.
People trying to own each other,
trying to change others
to fit their own desires,
trying to own their children.
People who call themselves yours
trying to get others to go their way.

I very seldom know
    whether I must do
    a certain thing or not.

I do not have head knowledge;
    I have *heart knowledge*,
    but people don't understand that.
Lord, do you?
Do I live close to you, Lord?
Do I, or is it my imagination?
I don't follow the rules
    of the church here on earth.
It doesn't matter which denomination
    I belong to.
I can't follow their do's and don'ts,
    their yea's and nay's.
Lord, am I wrong?

I see a gull in the sky,
    I think of you.
I watch the eagle soar
    and I think of you.
I find a grove of cedars
    and my thoughts go to you.
I hear the lake splash against the shore
    and I see your love.
I see a snake
    and my thoughts go to Moses
    and the serpent he had to lift high
    as you, the Son of Man,
    must be lifted up.
I see children and I ask,
    "Will they be yours, Lord?"
I meet older people and wonder,
    "Do they know your love?
    Have they been born again in your family?"

Surround and fill me with your love, Lord.
I don't like to feel like I do this morning.
So alone and a little lost.
I know it won't last,
        but today
            I am a lonely pilgrim
            in a ruthless world.

September 1, 1989

A new month and new days
        to serve you, Lord;
        to practice your presence
        to live for your glory
        to let you work through me
        to be open to your Holy Spirit
        to appreciate your love
        to see you in your mysteries
        to belong to you
        to follow you.

Whatever this month
        and these days bring,
        I pray that I will be
        open to your Holy Spirit.

September 25, 1989

King Solomon was given "one wish"
        by God, in a dream.
"Ask for whatever you want me to give you," God said.
Solomon asked for a "discerning heart,"
        or "wisdom."

Lord, as your servant,
    I, too, ask for a discerning heart.
People lie to me
    and I don't recognize the lie.
People trap me with falsehoods
    and I am caught before I know it.
Lord, even your people are,
    even I am,
    mired in subtleness,
    deceitfulness,
    jealousy,
    the need to outwit others,
    as we play psychological games,
    resort to lies to win;
    resort to sin to come out on top.

Lord, I need discernment and wisdom
    to recognize a lying heart,
    first in myself and then in others.

April 8, 1990   Palm Sunday

A beautiful day
    as I sit this morning on
    our back steps with our dog.

The fickle crowds calling,
    "Blessed is the King who comes
    in the name of the Lord"
    will, one week later,
    be crying out,
    "Crucify him."

Are we any different?
    No!
We are still fickle.

We say only what pleases us
    and what we think
        suits our own purposes.

May 9, 1990

O Lord,
    I am wandering away from you.
It is so difficult to keep this small ship
    on your course.
The winds of the adversary seem to take it
    and run with it,
        and I once again have to push
        and tug at the wheel
        to get it back.
Or do I have to do all this work?
Maybe I don't need to push
    and tug
        but give the wheel of my life
        to you.

I really can do nothing about it.
It's you who are the captain.
You are the owner of the store.
Perhaps I have taken my eyes off you,
    forgetting again that you are in charge.

Take the reins, Lord.
Fill me with your Holy Spirit.
Let the *I* in me fade
    and the *you* in me loom out
    through my every pore.

Let me be a sweet fragrance unto you.
Let me be "a fragrance of Christ to God
    among those who are being saved

and among those who are perishing."
    (2 Corinthians 2:15)

I need your Holy Spirit, Lord,
    to fill me constantly
        in my spirit,
        in my mind,
        in my body.
I need your Holy Spirit
    to take over every part of me.

Help me not to worry, Lord.
My stamina is not good.
I find it difficult to keep going.
I want to sleep and sleep.
Please, Lord, revive me.

May 24, 1990

I can hear the waves of Lake Superior
    caress the shoreline.
A nearby stream gurgles water
    down to the lake.
The animals quench their thirst
    in the abundance of spring water.
The deer, moose,
    black bears,
    silver foxes,
    and, deeper in the woods,
        the wolves,
    are active in the warmth
        of spring.
Birds are singing in the birch branches.
Gulls and blue jays screech
    their distinct songs.
Robins sing,

flickers flicker,
warblers warble,
and chickadees share their spring song.

Lord, what a beautiful morning!
The beauty of your creation
testifies to your love for it all.

Help us not to lose sight
of you, our creator.
We glory in our own creations.
We invent, we build,
thinking we have done something new,
when it is you
who established natural and scientific laws;
when it is you
who created the way for us to walk.
Lord, forgive our arrogance.
Bless us with your compassion and love
for we are the created,
never the creators.

August 30, 1990

There are, in churches today,
men's ways
women's ways
bishops' or district superintendents' ways,
traditional ways
pastors' ways.
I have found these ways
and these people,
while each has some of the truth,
are biased ways,
making it hard for me
to be content

in any denomination or church.

How we all need
　　God's direction
　　and submission
　　to his way.

September 3, 1990

The original church rule
　　which had to be broken and
　　　　cast aside
　　was circumcision,
　　　　the belief that all followers of Jesus
　　　　must be circumcised.
Paul set aside that rule, but
　　churches today, denominations today,
　　set up rules
　　　　for secondary points of belief,
　　　　for social conformity.
They have lists of
　　"Thou shalt nots,"
　　outward signs
　　　　for conformity
　　　　and membership.
Some churches say,
　　"Look how many conforming
　　members we have."

I am not to be part of that.
My soul is to be marked
　　only by the Lord Jesus Christ.
I must be free from the "circumcision rules"
　　and abandoned unto Christ,
　　marked by him
　　as a new creation.

53

September 11, 1990

Lord,
    I hate confrontation
    but if I don't stand up and confront,
    I get walked on.
This world we live in
    teaches it is okay to cheat,
        to push,
        to control–
    as long as we don't get caught.
This world says it is okay to calculate
    how far we can walk over another person
    before they scream.
Why is this, Lord?
What is it all about?

I respect others,
    but they don't respect me and my ways.
    (I guess I really am from another age.)
Christians and non-Christians alike
    may take advantage of people
    until they rebel,
        confront and
        scream in pain from the hurt.
I don't know how to cope
    in this world of dishonesty,
        lack of respect,
        jealousy and
        hatred.
Lord, if this is what I see,
    what do you see?

January 6, 1991

My Lord, I bow down before you,
    but the world, your world,
    battles Satan.
What have I seen on TV this morning?
Worship of other gods and goddesses;
    a goddess made of clay
        with grotesque breasts and buttocks
        named Mother Earth;
    women worshiping women,
    men worshiping men,
    church people worshiping evangelists,
        ministers and priests,
    lay people following their selfish ways,
    a world of people who
        are dead to the call of Jesus,
        blind to God's beauty,
        numb to the Holy Spirit.

Lord, how much longer
    can you tolerate us?
Lord, help us to recognize
    our sins
    and repent.
Put a protective shield around us.

January 28, 1991

It bothers me when people say,
    "God is in his heaven,
    and all is right with the world."
God is in more than his heaven.
He surrounds the world,
    acting as its protector.
All is not right with the world.

I see God tenderly
    holding the world
    as we fight,
    pollute and
    rock it to its very foundations.
I see tears flowing from his eyes, as he says,
    "They do not know what they do."

February 13, 1991

Lord,
    I give thanks that you care for me.
I know I'm not the best of humans.
I do not always have the best judgment, but
    right now
    it feels as though
    the people I care about
    are always correcting me
    and reproving me.
How come I am always wrong
    and they are always right?
Lord, I am feeling very low.
Do I bring out the worst in people?
Frequently, I think.
That is why I enjoy being alone with you.
You accept me the way I am.
How come they are all so smart
    and I am a dumb wife
    and mother
    and friend?

O Lord, I'm tired.
    I want to cry.
    I want to run
        —but I have a store to close out.

Help me, Lord.
Help me in all ways.
Let your Holy Spirit guide me in all that I do.
Help me to glorify you in everything I do.

February 17, 1991

This is one of the lowest days
    I have had in years.
I feel no one loves me.
I don't know why I am on earth.
I feel all religious practices are a fraud
    and mock our very existence.
We say we are happy
    but are we?
Right now I would like to shut everything and
    everybody
    out.

The questions I find myself asking today
    are ones teenagers,
    I suppose,
    ask
    —not questions sixty-year-olds are supposed to ask:
        Am I a puppet with an invisible person pulling my strings?
        Is God only a figment of my mind?
        Was I wrong about following God's direction?
        Were the stores only my own wishes and desires?
        How do I know there is truly a caring God?
        Do I only wish there was such a pie in the sky God?
I see on the news people all wishing for something better
    —embittered people.
Will I become bitter?
If what I've been taught is true,
    there is hope,
    there is no darkness.

(I simply don't care today.)

We are not going through tribulation, I'm told.
I think we are.
It's mental and soul tribulation
     and it's disastrous to our well-being.
Maybe all generations have gone through it.

Is there really a God who cares?
Or is it that we make him up for our own security?
Today, I think this is it.

Today, I have not gone to church.
I could not bear to listen
     to someone expound solely on their own ideas.

Life is a game with many players
     and I'm a loser
     and always have been.
Maybe all Christians are losers.

February 18, 1991

Derek called first and said,
     "We are concerned."
     And then Mom and Dad (my stepfather) called.

Last night I felt the Lord say,
     "You are not a loser.
     I have new plans for you.
     Walk on.
     The store must close so that new doors can open.
     Just take it one day at a time.
     Satan is trying to get at you.
     Are you going to let him win?"

"No," I answered
    and immediately my outlook changed.
Support in phone calls from my family lifted me.

The Lord says,
    "Come away my beloved.
    Climb the mountain with wings of an eagle.
    Fly up the mountainside and sit with me.
    Look down and see how far you can see.
    See the rivers fed by the mountain stream.
    Come higher and look below.
    What beauty!
    And how very far we can see.
    Over the hills, over the valleys."

When we are in a valley we cannot see over the hill.
We cannot see the river's source.
We cannot see the beaver's dam
    that is stopping the water in the stream,
    but the eagle can
    and so can the Lord.

God saw the dam building up
    log by log,
    obstacles put in the way
    of my spiritual journey with him.

God sees our problems
    and then he helps us see them too.

Truly Lord,
    you are the lover of my soul.
You alone are mine
    and I am yours.
You are not going to let
    another drag me down.

You alone gently remove me
from the clutches of the foreigner.
You alone throw your mantle of love
and warmth around me
until we become one,
as a husband and wife are one.

So we are or can be with the Lord.
This is the most beautiful of all relationships.
There are times of struggle and
missed communication
in a marriage
and so there are in the relationship
between the Lord and his beloved.
It is truly a personal, intimate relationship that we,
as believers,
can have with the Lord.

This morning I am truly renewed in his love
and I see myself fit,
vibrant
and full of his love.
He is my lover and I am his beloved.

March 7, 1991

The snow is falling.
It is very beautiful.
The lake is covered with snow and ice.
The fishermen are out
in their fishing shacks.

Lord,
I see you in the snow.
I see your beauty
in all our surroundings.

As the white snow falls,
    the earth is covered
    with a blanket of softness,
    pure and white.
I am reminded of the cover you have for us;
    a cover that is white,
    beautiful,
    showing no blemish.
Your suffering on the cross, dear Jesus,
    your forgiveness of my sins,
    makes me white as snow
    in the eyes of our Father.
Lord, wrap me in that
    snow white blanket
    of forgiving love.

April 12, 1991

Springtime has brought
    juncos, gulls, ducks,
    sparrows, loons,
    and many small birds to our lake.
This morning there is
    a gray mourning dove
    at our little creek.
How I love mourning doves.
Their voices are so sweet to my ears.
So often God brings
    birds into my life
    when I need encouragement
    or I need to know his presence
    is with me.
The mourning dove
    symbolizes peace in this place,
    the presence of my lover, the Lord.

"Peace I leave with you;
My peace I give to you;
    not as the world gives,
    do I give to you," Jesus says.
        (John 14:27)
A peace that wells up
    from within.
May your peace radiate through me,
    and be seen both by my friends
    and by people who do not know me.
May I be like that little
    gray-brown dove,
    unnoticeable
    but
    quietly,
    simply
    spreading your peace.

August 31, 1991

No matter whether we are homosexual or heterosexual,
    we must be disciplined.
We must learn control over our actions,
    our desires,
    our ego,
    our will.
We must obey God's will for ourselves.

No church can do this for us,
    nor any group of Christians.
No one except us,
    with the help
    of the Holy Spirit.

Lord, how do we learn about ourselves
    and what you have created us to be?

What our potential is in you?
And why can't we see how great we have been created,
    how beautifully unique,
    as different as snowflakes
    but in similar molds
    and bodies?

September 2, 1991

As I prepare soup for lunch,
    I watch our three weekend houseguests
    out on the porch and swing
        playing and laughing,
        at forty-plus years of age,
        like little kids.
Last night we shared
    our pasts,
    our families,
    our hurts,
    our joys.
We laughed and cried,
    realizing that God
    has brought us through life
        to this healing relationship
    in this, our home.
When we moved to this home,
    John and I prayed
    that it would
    become a place of refuge,
    a spot for people to find
    a Christlike atmosphere,
    a place of rest,
    of God's love
    and God's guidance.
Thank you, God,
    for prayer abundantly answered.

Thank you
    for the privilege
    of making soup
    for lunch.

October 26, 1991

As Jesus said to Peter in John 21:15,
    "Feed my lambs,"
    so I hear him say,
    "I've been bringing my lambs to you.
    Do you love me?
    Then take care of my sheep."

O yes,
    and I am like Peter.
I don't really want the boredom
    of being at home
    for the lambs
    to come.
But,
    I must.
That is where the Father wants me.
By waiting in one place where the lambs can find me.
    His lambs.
The hardest thing for me right now
    is waiting for God,
    waiting patiently
    with
    nothing
    exciting
    to
    do.
Like being home with small children,
    being the caretaker
    but *waiting patiently,*

that is my work.

The lambs who come are mature in the world
    but they are tiny babies in the Lord.

Patience is the word.
So hard for me.
O Lord,
    give me quiet patience.

Is this meekness?
"Blessed are the meek, for they will inherit the earth,"
    Jesus says in Matthew 5:5.
I guess this is what the Lord is teaching me.
O Lord,
    you always turn things backwards in me
    and then I feel you
    laughing with love
    and it is a funny joke on me.

I have been trying to teach your lambs meekness
    and you are teaching me meekness,
    and patience.

You say,
    "Feed my lambs that surround you,"
    but Lord,
    I need the formula directions
    so they won't get indigestion.

October 27, 1991

There is a passion for souls
    that does not spring from God
    but from the desire to make converts
    to our point of view.

January 5, 1992

I must remember
    that not only I
    but many others
    work to further
    the kingdom of God on earth.
We are each unique in his family.
We all have different jobs,
    different spaces to conquer for him.
Our Father does not intend
    to tire us out
    but to have us rest in him.
He gives us time to be quiet
    time to rest
    time to work—very hard.
He does not want us
    to get all worked up,
    upset,
    about other's problems,
    problems we can do nothing about.
I don't know about others,
    but I have come to realize
    if something is right for me to do
    then I should do it,
    regardless of whether or not others see it
    or accept it.
So, not only I,
    but many others,
    work as we are led
    for the kingdom of God on earth.

May 7, 1992

The cost of being
    a disciple of the Lord's

is high.
He asks us all,
  women,
  men,
  and children alike
to see that
  the quality of Jesus' righteousness,
  the way in which he lived,
  the acceptance of the cross,
  and the magnificence of his resurrection,
  make him surely,
  certainly,
  the Son of God.
He wants us all
  to personally receive him
  as Lord and Savior,
  to be first in our lives
  before
        mothers and fathers
        husbands and wives
        sons and daughters
        relatives and friends.

The cost of being
  a disciple of the Lord
  is high.

May 18, 1992   Marney's Psalm
(read at her memorial services)

A lot has been done in the garden
  as far as clean up goes,
  but it has been cold and wet.

I've planted my moss baskets
  with miniature roses

to hang on the front porch.

The birds have been beautiful:
    red polls, grackles,
    indigo buntings,
    and, this morning, an oriole.

How I thank God!

I dared to hope the orioles would come.
I do hope they stay.
I wonder if he is a scout bird.
I've oranges out.
He is back again,
    making a pig out of himself.
How exciting!

I am feasting on the beauty of the bird.
What a gift from God!
Blue jays, chickadees,
    warblers, finches.
O, thanks to God!
The trees are truly full of birds.
I give thanks to God!

September 6, 1992

Lord, my tongue wags too much.
When I am hurt,
    my tongue wags.
When I am upset,
    my tongue wags.
When I am frustrated,
    my tongue wags.
Even when I need to be quiet,
    my tongue wags.

My tongue wags
    with little restraint
    even to family members
    about family members.

Lord, help me to quiet my tongue.
Give me wisdom
    and discernment
    in what I think
    and say.

January 5, 1993

There is no reward
    to show people.
There is no accomplishment
    to tell about.
There is nothing to claim
    aloud.

There is only
    a wonderful sense
        of knowing he is here with me,
    a security when the Lord
        wraps his loving blanket around me,
    a peace
        when he calms my anxieties,
    a voice saying,
        "Be still and know that I am God."

January 6, 1993

When you live with a person
    and have an intimate relationship with her/him,
    it is said you begin to look like that person.

69

If this is true,
    I hope the countenance
    of Jesus Christ
    shines through me.

Late January 1993

I remember
    a lily
    blooming in a muddy field
    on the side of a small mountain
    in Okinawa.
It bloomed pure white
    in the middle
    of the dirtiest mud
    I have ever seen.
It was a beautiful sight.

I hope I am like that lily
    for people to see
    for God to see
    for God to use.

April 22, 1993

Did people think Jesus
    and his followers
    were a cult
    when he lived on earth?
If I had been on earth then
    would I have been a follower?
Jesus' "cult" was different.
He did not point to himself
    as cult leaders do.

He pointed to his Father,
	to God, our Father
		and Creator.

Would I have seen
	the difference?
Would I have been a follower?

April 23, 1993

I've been thinking of the time
	when I was locked in the hospital
	for three weeks.
It was a very degrading experience
	but I had become addicted to the drugs
	that had been prescribed
	for my migraine headaches.
The sooner I came to this realization,
	the sooner I started to heal.

That all happened in 1980
	and I was forty-seven years old.
It was a very uncomfortable situation but,
	looking back on it,
	it was where God wanted me.
He did not use only his own children
	to help me.
God used many people to help me
	see myself in a new light.
I found out that
	with his help,
	I was responsible for me.
Not John's help,
	not my children's,
	not some other wonderful Christian's help,
	but his,

71

through his Holy Spirit.

God, through his Holy Spirit,
    taught me I had defiled his temple
    which is in me.
If he had not turned me from the path I was on,
    I would not be here today.
Since then,
    step by step,
    he has taught me
    that he wants
    a personal relationship
    with me.
He wants to live within me
    and he wants to clean out
    the junk in my life.
My eyes must be kept on him.
I cannot dictate to him
    where I will live
    or what I will do.
I've had to break a lot of ties,
    drop a lot of people
    when they interfered
    with his will for my life.

Since that time in April 1980
    my life has become so exciting;
    an adventure with God.

"He lives, He lives,
    Christ Jesus lives today!
He walks with me and talks with me
    along life's narrow way.
He lives, He lives,
    salvation to impart!
You ask me how I know He lives?
    He lives within my heart,"

Alfred Ackley wrote in *He Lives*
and it's become my song, too.

Surely I was a child of God,
    long, long before 1980,
    1934 to be exact,
    but I have learned a lot
    through my time in that hospital
    and now.
My relationship with the triune God
    is one that enables me to say:
    "I can do everything through him."
        (Philippians 4:13)

June 3, 1993

This morning
    there are clouds,
    but the sun is peeking through
    here and there.
The birds!
Their voices are beautiful!
I wonder, do the birds know
    they sing praises
    to our, and their,
    Father God?
Yesterday,
    a bird I did not see
    trilled and sang wonderfully.
I've not heard anything like it.
I don't know what kind of bird it was,
    but probably
    it was a dull, brown bird.
Sometimes it is not
    the beautiful, colorful birds
    that have the sweetest sounds

but the dull, brown birds.

God's children are like that, too.
It's the dull background person
    who sings the sweetest
    songs to God's ears.
Christians who serve up front are needed,
    but the lady who washes clothes,
        the people who are neither
        seen nor heard by many,
    often sing the most beautiful
        songs to God.

August 31, 1993

"Let us fix our eyes on Jesus,
    the author and perfecter of our faith,
    who for the joy set before him endured the cross,"
        Paul says in Hebrews 12:2.

Jesus' joy
    was in doing the will of the Father,
    even unto the cross.

Joy does not mean
    happiness
    as we use it today,
    as many misuse it.

Joy in Christ's sense
    is in knowing that
    we are doing
    the will of the Father.

Joy comes when you and I
    are obedient to God's will for us.

In doing God's will
    there is peace in our soul,
    inner peace.
In doing God's will
    there is *joy*.

September 28, 1993

You know, Lord,
    it is so much fun
    working in secret with you.
I love it
    when people come into the store and say,
    "It is so peaceful here."
I think in astonishment,
    "Really?"
But then I remember,
    "Of course it is
    because you are here."
I am happy customers feel your presence.
I am happy our store shines forth
    your peace.

What is really fun too, Lord,
    are the times I talk about you
    without thinking about it
      or even realizing it,
    your Spirit moving in me,
    knowing what each person needs to hear.
Often I'm surprised at what comes out of me.

Lord, loving you is fun!

January 11, 1994

Lord,
    may the holy ground
    around our small church
    come alive for your glory.
May a sanctuary
    rise on that land.
May we become and be known as
    a group of *on fire* believers.
Lord, I see a sanctuary built of logs rising up,
    a gateway to Two Harbors.
I see rejoicing in your people,
    a congregation full of vigor and vitality for you.
Satan will not destroy
    this family of believers.
All power from you will break through,
    for you are our God.
You will go forward with us
    like a flame at night
    and a soft cloud by day.
You will direct our paths
    into your righteous ways.
O Lord,
    how great Thou art.

December 3, 1993

Yesterday I worked
    in the church nursery.
It reminded me that
    to reach
    young children
    you have to
    get down
    on the floor

and play,
do what they are doing.
You can't just sit in a chair
to communicate with them.

Isn't that how we reach
all people?
Do what they do,
be active "on their floor."

Isn't that what you did, God,
to reach us?
You came to us
at our level.
You sent Jesus
to raise us up,
to bring us into your arms.

February 8, 1994

When we give ourselves
over to the Lord
to be made holy,
it is not a quick change.
It is a day-by-day change.
It happens gradually.
I change slowly,
very slowly...
but I do change.

April 13, 1994

I awoke this morning at five to rain.
The gulls and birds are also awake.
The gulls are noisy.

The robins and song sparrows
    are singing too.
What beautiful music—
    the sweet sounds of spring.
We're all in your care, Lord.

It's wonderful to be able to come to you
    in thought and spirit
    even before my eyes are open.
I don't have to get a lamb to sacrifice
    or travel to a holy place.
I'm able to talk to you
    anytime
    anywhere
    because you're with me.
Lord, it is living in this intimate,
    personal relationship with you
    that sustains me.

June 23, 1994

Sin is a choice in our lives
    not just a shortcoming in our character.
Sin is blatant mutiny
    against God
    by each of us.
Either sin or God
    must die.
If sin rules,
    God will be killed in us.
If God rules,
    sin will die.
We must
    bring ourselves to realize
    that sin kills
        and is the source

of the grief and sorrow
in our lives.

August 20, 1994

How often we hear
   "Bloom where you are planted"
      as a trite phrase,
but in our world,
   in God's world,
      his garden is large
      and "the workers are few."
So God needs each worker,
   needs us
   to work in his garden
      in our spot.
At special times
   we may be called
   to share experiences–
      gardening techniques,
      joys of success,
      sorrows of failure.
We may even travel
   to faraway gardens
   to help or to learn,
but then we must go back
   to our corner of the garden,
   for it needs lots of care.
As God calls
   we must respond to his call.

Lord, make me a true and faithful gardener.

September 9, 1994

The world is full of bluffing
    and bluffers;
    full of deceiving
    and deceivers.
When I have to deal
    with myself,
    I want to be honest.
I want to know
    my true qualities.
I want honest friends;
    people who are true to themselves
    and me.
When I am honest with myself,
    I can be honest with others
    and God.
Lord, when I bluff myself or others,
    cause the Holy Spirit
    to catch me
    and rebuke me.

September 27, 1994

If a church leader or pastor
    is a weak, uncertain Christian,
    it is hard for a congregation
        to see through the veneer
        of Christian bravado.
By tradition, congregations
    give authority and leadership positions
    to people with Christian education.
We follow trustingly
    and then are surprised
    when they fail us.

God's people
    need his discernment
    in following.
Ultimately our trust
    must rest in
        God, the Father,
        Jesus Christ, his Son,
        and in the Holy Spirit
           who leads us.

October 13, 1994

Another week half done.
The weeks fly by
    as if there are no weeks
    but only one day
    with naps.

February 10, 1995

The Episcopal *Book of Common Prayer*
    has many beautiful songs of praise
    to our triune God.
The Evangelical Church has a freedom
    and spontaneity of worship
    fit for our king.
If only we could put the two together!
Why do we go to extremes,
    each throwing the other's
    baby out with the bath water?
The praises to God from each service
    are the same:
    Praising Father, Son and Spirit,
    praising the triune God.
O, God, help us by the power of the living God.

April 6, 1995

When I plan a room, design it,
    I see it all mentally in my mind's eye
    months or even a year ahead
    of the finished work.
When it is structurally finished
    someone will turn to me and say,
    "It's beautiful.
    Is it as nice as you thought it would be?"
    "Yes, it is, for I *saw it* in my mind long ago,
        and now it is finished."

I wonder if this is not how God is
    about our lives.
God plans, works out the details,
    and rejoices when the plan is fulfilled.
God, the Father, worked out a plan for Jesus, his Son,
    and when that plan was fulfilled
    in a glorious way he, too, said,
    "It is finished!"

June 13, 1995

I cannot,
    I must not,
    project my experiences with God
    on others.
The way that I am used by Jesus Christ
    will not be the way
    others are used.
On the other hand,
    I must be careful
    not to let others project onto me
    their experiences with Christ.

I love to ask God,
    "But how about him or her?"
God smiles in gentle rebuke and says,
    "I will lead that one in my way.
    Only be concerned about my way for you."
Am I following your way for me?
Help me, Lord,
    to be part of your glory.

June 30, 1995

There is a woman,
    I know,
    not gifted with words,
    of average intelligence,
    with a sense of humor.
She is not anyone special.
No one will write books or stories
    about her.
But she is full of God's love.
She has security only in him.
She gives her all to him:
    time
    energy
    devotion
    and her widow's mite.
She is number one
    in God's kingdom.

I would like to be that woman!

September 24, 1995

In the store,
    as I put ribbons on packages
        to decorate them,
    I am sharing a small
        touch of God's beauty
        with our customers.
Each bow is tied
    with love
    and a silent prayer.

Later

I am who I am
    because God made me
    for his purpose.
I am where I am
    because God placed
    me here
    for his purpose.
I am to be me.
I was not born
    for any other century.
I was born for now.
This is who I am
    and this is where God has placed me.
As I praise Jesus
    and thank him
    for the hope he has given me,
may I respond to the challenge
    of this place and time.

October 31, 1995

How often do I think,
    "Why do I keep my eyes
        on Jesus?
    He has not come.
    I cannot see him
        except with the
        eyes of my soul."
And yet, as the flame
    grows dim,
    it is fanned alive again
    by his Holy Spirit.
I may grow weak
    and almost faithless,
    but he will not let me go.
I am flamed alive
    by his sweet
        holy presence in my life,
    by that presence
        which moves me
        to become
    a glowing candle
        for God, my Father.

June 19, 1996

Lord, my ministry
    is not flashy.
It still is
    to live for your glory
    and the good of many.
I live struggling
    with each day as it comes,
    counting on your Holy Spirit
    to fill me and lead me.

May I live with your love and light
    so filling me that
    your way overflows from me
        to be seen
        by others.

Lord, my way
    is flawed by many mistakes.
Often I speak out as I see things
    and that is not popular with people.
I am impatient at times.
I don't tolerate "hoodwinkers."
Those who bluff their way through life
    are obnoxious.
Lord, return truth, directness and honesty
    to your people.

July 8, 1996

In 1950
    girls were to smile sweetly,
    be pleasing,
    do what was expected.
No straying outside the lines.
Suppress your mind,
    otherwise you will sour everyone.
In other words,
    in all of life,
    keep every hair in place.
Be: pleasing
    demure
    compliant
    conforming
    docile
    and sweet.

Obtain what you need,
    want,
    by charm
    not by being open and direct.
Be poised on the outside
    regardless of the chaos inside.
Above all, smile.

Walking With a Calling

June 30, 1985

Applying to become an ordained deacon
    in my church
    is overwhelming me.
It's a long process to apply
    and a three-year course of study.
Even as I doubt,
    I feel God saying,

"I've prepared you for this.
Go ahead and I'll be with you
    and those who interview you.
Walk on, walk on,
    and be amazed at what I will do with you
        —for I am your God—
    you are my servant.
I've chosen you, and
    though you have no degrees,
    you have great learning.
You have learned through pain,
    physically,
    mentally,
    spiritually.
Go ahead my beloved child.
    I will be with you.
    I love you.
There are things in your family,
    you have need to deal with.
As you have read of my prophet Hosea,
    so shall you be.

"Walk on, go on,
    I am with you forever.
Reach out to my children
    but do not let them stall you.
    You shall walk on.

Some will walk beside you.
  My servant, John, will hold your hand.
  You are together one flesh.
  I have joined you both into one.
    You are my beloved.
    You complement each other.
    Walk together.

"There will be more storms,
  more sorrow.
I will look after the children
  you have borne and raised.
Walk on; don't get discouraged.
You have your love for each other
  and your love for me
  and, in return,
    you have my love always
    until the end.
You will never die.
You will live with me.
  Walk on, walk on.

"Walk on my child.
Weep with those who mourn
  but walk on, walk on.
Your children will follow.
They will become strong in me.
  Walk on, walk on.

"I am with you always and with your children's children.
You have taught them well.
They will bear fruit for me.
  Walk on, walk on.

"Leave them in my hands.
I will love them and care for their needs
  and your daughter

will produce my fruit too, definitely.
She will learn to trust me completely.

"My angels surround you all like Elisha.
You are all surrounded by heavenly armies.
You will tread on the enemies.
You will not be stopped.

"Walk on my beloved child,
    walk on.
You will learn of my ways for you.
Have no fear.
Walk on, walk on.

"I am with you always even to the end of the world.
We will then live together
    forever and ever.
You will be united with loved ones
    who have prepared the way for you
    with their love for me.
Walk on my beloved, walk on.
You are my child.

"Look not to each other's past sins.
    They are forgiven.
Grow in me.
    Let me fill your lives with my grace.
Be full in me.
Lean not unto your own understanding.
I am all knowledge,
    all understanding,
    all compassion,
    all love.
Grow in me and I will grow in you.

"Walk on, walk on.
    You are my beloved child.

Grow beyond those around you who gape in awe.
    I have raised you up.
    Follow me.
    I will guide you.
    I am the Holy Triune God.
    I have chosen you.

"Wonder not at others' pain.
I use them, too, in my kingdom.
        I love you all with an everlasting love.
        Do not be afraid to
            walk on, walk on."

I have complete peace.
    I will walk on—
    as he leads me.

September 5, 1985

Thanks for John, Lord.
I could not prepare to be a deacon without his help.
He has been given a fine mind.

Our time of love together has been beautiful;
    a time of building a new life together.

Lord, thanks for John.

I am a woman who has been greatly blessed.
I thank you for my parents and their teachings,
    and for the love of grandparents
    who taught me your ways
    that I might go even further.

Help us to enable our children,
    and their children,

to learn of your ways
   so your kingdom will flourish here on earth.

Undated, 1985

It does not matter whether I am a deacon
   or a layperson.
My ministry is to reach and help
   those I come in contact with:
      help with daily living
      help to a deeper Christian faith.
It may be as a shopkeeper,
   a layperson,
   a homemaker,
   or a deacon.

God has given me many gifts
   to help me serve him through Jesus Christ, my Lord.
As I meet new challenges
   the triune God meets my needs.
When I take action on a challenge,
   his spirit is there.
Sometimes I am surprised and amazed
   at what God can do through me
   if I am obedient to him.

As deacon or layperson
   I need to:
      think big
      think wide
      think positively
      think love
      think service
      and never underestimate the power of God.

January 10, 1987

Lord, these exams, tests and paperwork
    have to be done
    for my preparation
    to become a deacon.

Lord, is that where I am to be?

I need your Spirit to show me,
    the same Spirit that is in Jesus Christ,
    the Spirit that feeds me today.
He helps me transcend to the highest places.

How much do I *use* this Holy Spirit?
Do I let him fill me?
Or do I limit his power within me?

Sadly, I limit the Spirit!

I must not limit the Holy Spirit within me.
I must let him flow through me to others.
I must act on the whispers of his voice.

Fill me with your Spirit, Christ my Lord.
May your Spirit guide me
    guide my paths
    guide my tongue
    guide my love
    guide my ways
    guide my thoughts
    always.

With the power of your Holy Spirit
    mountains can be moved,
    the impossible made possible,
    and your peace become my peace.

March 24, 1987

Tonight the second council on ministries
    takes place.
My second interview on the road
    to becoming a deacon.
Lord, I am trusting
    that you will
    give me your words,
    that I will be filled
    with your Spirit.
Enable me!

August 9, 1987

Lord, am I not to be ordained a deacon?
Is it not your will that
    I should be ordained
    by men and women?
I know that I am ordained by you,
    to *bloom* for you
    wherever I am,
    but if I am not to be ordained, Lord,
    why did I go through
    all that?
You know, Lord,
    I don't have the credentials of this world
    and it is hard
    not to have something!
But, every time I have gone ahead
    with the deacon program
    there has been something
    to hold me back...
    M.R.'s illness,
    Amy's health,
    my dad,

me...
It is so discouraging
    to feel
    I have finished
    nothing.
Matter of fact,
    it is painful.
What am I to do?
Father,
    help me to accept
    your way.

April 23, 1989

I would have liked to be
    an ordained deacon, to be a "Rev,"
    but you did not have that for me.
The studies...yes.
The formal ordination...no.

I study for each new challenge and opportunity:
    my teaching
    my Red Cross responsibilities in Okinawa
    my refugee work
    my sexuality counseling
    my stores.
They have added up to
    knowledge and skills
    more than equivalent
    to most university degrees,
    but not recognized by others.

I do not have the honor
    higher education on earth brings.
I do not have the earthly rewards
    of human achievement.

It hurts, Lord.
Sometimes I cry
    but my hand is in your hand
    and you pull me on.

Walking With Family

January 23, 1981

John joined me this morning
    as I spent time with God.
    It was difficult to share
    some of my feelings
        of praise and thankfulness.
Then a quiet rest came over
    both John and me.
Peace and rest
    seems to be soaking
    into both of us.
We need closeness
    with each other
    and with you
    very much.

Undated, 1985

John and I dated on and off
    for four years
    before we became engaged.
A lot of prayer went into our union.
I was a Plymouth Brethren girl,
    a small sect
    that tried, as much as possible,
        to follow the early church
    of the disciples.
It was a big deal
    for someone to marry
    outside the Brethren
        and John was United Church (Methodist)
        (his father a minister to boot).
As a result,
    John was not the man
    my parents preferred.

I was going against the accepted way.

One day my aunt came to visit.
A beautiful woman of God,
    she was keenly aware
    of spiritual matters.
She called me to her room and said,
    "Marney,
    I know you have a young man
    whom you love
        and I've been told to tell you
        to go ahead and marry him,
            even though you will have a hard time
            with your parents and grandparents."
She must have talked to them
    because they agreed to the marriage,
    but my father!
I was not sure he would give me away
    even until the day of the wedding,
    May 29, 1954.

Undated, 1985

When the Holy Spirit came into my life
    (and I recognized the coming),
    he was a bright light.

I was fighting in a nightmare;
    something was trying to keep me in a dark hole,
    weird forces were holding me down.
Suddenly a beautiful voice said,
    "Take my hand."
I knew it was Jesus' hand.
There was another hand and Jesus said,
    "Take it."
It was my husband's hand.

Jesus said,
 "Hold tight to John's hand.
 I've given him to you as a helpmate.
 I, Jesus, will always hold on to you."

A beautiful light has remained with me always,
 the light that shone that day.

July 14, 1985

O Lord, my heart is not lifted up
 (as a matter of fact, my soul is weeping—
 so much death, sin and sorrow).
Yet I know, God my Father,
 you need me to see the pain in the world.

How your heart must ache, Lord,
 when you see how we hurt each other!
How your soul must weep!

"Why, my children, why do you destroy each other
 without even knowing what you do?
I, your Lord God, grieve for you.
 I put a flower in your hand,
 and you crush it."

July 14, 1985

I wonder why marriage
 is supposed to be so great?
Is your partner there when you
 need him?
Hardly ever!
But I am supposed to be there
 when my partner needs me.

He thinks "it" is a gift
    from him to me.
How ridiculous!
Sometimes I think a nunnery
    would be the answer.

Undated, 1985

God speaks,
    "Women must learn to be totally giving of themselves
        to their husbands.
No excuses.
No doubts.
Just relaxing and letting love
    flow back and forth.
Don't jab each other verbally.
Don't criticize.
Love one another fully and intimately
    then, together,
        you will know how to love me."

Undated, 1985

In 1967,
    John came home from work
    and said to me,
    "Marney, how would you like to move
        to Okinawa?"
I answered,
    "Where? Oklahoma?"
    "No," John said. "Okinawa."
    "Where is that?"
John got the world map out
    and showed me.
    It was south of Japan.

106

I said, "No!"
John went ahead and sent in his papers
Somehow they got lost
    and another person got the job.
Relief!
But God wasn't finished with the matter.
He started to deal with me
    and brought me to my knees.
I was being asked by him
    to give up
    my materialistic self.
After many months of fighting God
    I said, "Yes, God,
    I will go wherever you want
        to send me.
    You can have my house,
        my kitchen, everything."
John's papers were found within two days.
We left in June of 1968
    for two years.

John's job was a military, government and
    University of Hawaii position,
    setting up a residency program
    for Japanese and Okinawan doctors.
I worked as an occupational therapist
    with paraplegics and leprosy patients
    and later for the Red Cross
    and wounded Vietnam veterans.

What can I say about an experience
    that changed my life?
I learned to praise God.
I became very dependent on him
    for everything.
I learned to follow him first,
    before family opposition,

before material needs.
I marvel at it now.

September 6, 1985

My omnipotent Father says to me:
    "Give your whole attention to me
        as you do to your husband.
    Let everything else go from your mind.
        Dwell completely in me, your God.
        Let me fill you with my Spirit.
    Just as your marriage is enriched spiritually
        by the love you have for John,
            so concentrate and intensify your love
            for me, your God.
    Don't let thoughts of other people
        or other things
        come into our time together.
    This you are learning
        in your love for your husband.
    Go further, zero in on me,
        your heavenly bridegroom.

    "Just as you give your total mind,
        body and spirit
        to your beloved husband, John,
            in intercourse,
        so I,
        your God,
        need that intensity of love, too.

    "Learn this pure love together
        then share it with others as my Spirit leads.
    Share it with me.
    I want the same kind of love
        you are learning to give each other.

Practice it.
Practice it.
Others will see your love and,
by example,
learn how to love their spouses
as they learn to love me more fully.
You and John are learning how
to be completely one in each other
so that you are able to be completely one in me."

November 25, 1985

We are in the throes of moving (by December 15)
from Duluth,
north,
to Two Harbors.
Our new home will not be ready.
There is an aura of uncertainty
about our lives.

John and M.R. each went out in a *huff*.
This is supposed to be a day off for John
but he is doing surgery.
Every room in the house is a mess
and I need his help.
I am in a mess at the bank.

God?

I hear you say
within the depths of my soul,
"Be still and know that I am God."

Quietly I ask
Have you ever let me down? No!
I may not know your way now

but you have a purpose for us
and our new home.
Do my journals not show
your constant love and caring
over the past sixteen years
since we lived in Okinawa?
Indeed, over the past fifty-four years,
and even my whole life?
Have I not always been surrounded by your love?

Where is my home?
My home is
in you
in purity
in knowledge
in patience
in kindness
in the Holy Spirit
in genuine love
in the word of truth
and in your power.

"Be still Marney. Fear not," you answer.
"I am with you.
I am the true Father.
I have waited patiently
for you to come to me.
I am with you always."

September 25, 1986

Jesus warns me to,
"Beware of practicing your righteousness
before men to be noticed by them;
otherwise you have no reward with your Father
who is in heaven." (Matthew 6:1)

O, my Lord, let me not come off as a *holy snob*.
Help me not to boast before men and women.

But sometimes I feel as though I want the world
    to know the good I've done for someone else.
This, I think, is a natural thing.

To say,
    "Hey world, look what I've done for so and so."

Sometimes when another Christian gets gifts of praise
    I want to say,
    "Lord, why not me?"

It is very hard to sit by, still and quiet,
    unnoticed by others.
    But that is what Jesus is talking about in this reading.

Later

Father Brennan
    at the Benedictine Center
    is a quadriplegic from multiple sclerosis.
He says he didn't realize how much his hands *helped* him to sin.

When you sit and think of all our hands do:
    pushing unneeded food into us...
    enabling us to smoke...
    and drink...
In almost everything we do,
    our hands are helping us to do it—
    good or bad.

Perhaps this is why Jesus said,
    "Do not let your left hand know what the right hand is doing."

March 9, 1987

When all is said and done,
    I can pray for family and friends
    without knowing all the details.
I only need to know that prayer,
    special prayer,
    is needed.
Why is it such a struggle, then,
    to stop myself from picking up the phone
    and getting the latest scoop?
I can use
    the telephone as a useful tool
    or as an aid for
    my sharp tongue.
This has truly been a struggle for me
    over the years:
    addiction to the telephone!
Gossip becomes the source of much harm
    especially now when it can spread
    long distances in a matter of minutes.
Used with love, the telephone
    brings families together.
Used correctly, it can be a lifesaver.

After thinking this through
    I am over my need to call for details.
Now I can pray.

May 15, 1987

"I waited patiently for the Lord:
    And He inclined to me,
    and heard my cry." (Psalm 40:1)

I did wait for the Lord

through many years of migraine headaches,
and he did hear me
after a number of years;
most likely he heard me throughout
and I did not hear his reply.

"He brought me up out of the pit of destruction,
    out of the miry clay;
And He set my feet upon a rock
    making my footsteps firm.
And He put a new song in my mouth,
    a song of praise to our God." (Psalm 40:2-3)

This is all true.
The Lord did exactly this.
My familial migraine headaches,
    present from childhood,
    controlled my life for more than ten years.
In 1980, hooked on prescription painkillers,
    God sent a physician
    who cared for me as a person,
    as a child of God.
He admitted me to a pain control center.

During a hellish night of withdrawal,
    God sent an angel
    in the form of a nurse
    to my side.
Through the agony and pain she prayed for me
    and during that night
    the light hit me!
God literally
    brought me up out of the pit of destruction
    and set my feet upon a rock.

Now I sing a new song of praise.
I know the Lord in a new way,

a completely new way.

Thank you, Lord, a thousand times
    that you
    "Inclined to me
    and heard my cry."

*Note: Marney's headaches became infrequent, two or three times
a year, for the rest of her life.*

August 11-12, 1987

Praise the Lord, O my soul.

"This is the day the Lord has made;
let us rejoice and be glad in it."
    (Psalm 118:24)

Shortly after I wrote that
    a lady called me
    to say Shanghai, our dog,
        had been killed on the highway.
How could that happen?
So easily.
Shang did not want to stay home.
He was unhappy being chained or shut up.

How I miss him.

Shang was loved not only by us
    but by our friends, neighbors,
        and the guests at the hotel near our house.
Shang was a very special dog.
He loved people
    and really thought he was a person.
He was my companion.

He traveled in the car with me
    and waited patiently for my return.
When John was at the hospital at night,
    he stayed by my side,
    a true watchdog.

How I miss him!

When I came home tonight
    no one was there to greet me.
There was no one wanting me
    to leave some cereal in my bowl.
Shang always knew when I was coming
    to the bottom of my bowl
    by the clicking of the spoon.

There are so many memories of Shang.
Today I have been grieving his loss.
How I loved him.
Five years old and a beautiful dog,
    beautiful temperament.
The loss of him is great.
There will be other dogs
    but never another Shanghai.

Praise the Lord, for the Lord is good.
His mercies endure forever.

August 16, 1987

Beijing, a purebred cocker spaniel,
    has entered our lives
    and quickly is a member of our family.

September 7, 1987

To my children:

Each of us is Christian.
Each of us is in a different denomination.
I wonder why?
Over the years Dad and I have never told you
    what denomination to belong to.
How could we?
I do not believe that any Christian denomination
    has the "right way"
    or the "wrong way."
I have found over the years
    that my need for spiritual growth
    has taken me out of certain church groups
    and into others which have met my needs.
This is the way I hope
    each of you will look at yourselves.
You are held accountable
    only for your own Christian growth.
Too often I have found myself
    looking at another and saying,
    "My way is better than yours."
Is it?
How do I know
    what God has for another child of his?
Even though each of you is our child
    here on earth,
    there is a greater relationship
    that we share.
We are brothers and sisters in Jesus' family.
We must not judge but support one another.
It is easy to look at each other and be critical—
    don't!
Just be sure you know the "right way" for you!

God has allowed each of us
  to grow in Christ in special ways
  but always in God, the Father,
    God, the Son,
    God, the Spirit.

December 14, 1987

Marney Ruth was married to Bill Crandall on December 12, 1987.
Two or three weeks ago
  I knew there was no way
  I could look after every detail.
There was only one who could
  so I *gave* the wedding to the Lord,
  trusting that all involved in the plans
  would have the same peace and calm
  that I had.

The wedding went beautifully.
I think everyone had lots of fun.

Some people said,
  "It was a royal wedding,"
  perhaps not realizing
  the deeper meaning of what they said.
For truly it was a royal wedding.
The host was the "King of kings."

Lord, this morning I ask for your
  continued blessing
  on Marney Ruth and Bill
  and on us all.

February 8, 1988

A new week begins.

"Create in me a clean heart, O God,
And renew a steadfast spirit within me.
Restore to me the joy of Thy salvation,
And sustain me with a willing spirit.
Then I will teach transgressors Thy ways,
And sinners will be converted to Thee,"
    I pray to God with David in his psalm.
       (51:10, 12, 13)

Sitting at the dining room windows looking out
    I see and hear little birds
    busy eating the sunflower seeds
    I have thrown on top of the snow for them.
With the whiteness of the snow
    and the blue of the lake,
    it is all so very beautiful.

My thoughts turn to the cycle of seasons,
    each season with its own beauty,
    then to the seasons of my lifetime.

I am fast approaching the winter season of my life
    and it, too, is a beautiful time
    (even though the society I live in does not make it beautiful).

But maybe it is the most beautiful time;
    snow white hair,
    I can wear colors I could not wear before,
    and though my body is not too beautiful,
    it is a body that comforts grandchildren and holds others close
       upon pillow breasts.

As I think upon the mystery of seasons

I wonder what my Father God
has in store for me as spring returns.
I hear him say, "Wait and see."

February 14, 1988

Praise the Lord for he is truly wonderful.
He is mighty.
He is a true God of love
He truly cares for his children.

Amy, my granddaughter,
    has been in hospital in Hamilton, Ontario,
    for bleeding—hemorrhaging.
Her liver is giving out.

Two nights ago
    I talked with her mother, Deb,
    for a long time.
I was concerned for them when I hung up.
I prayed,
    petitioning God for a liver for Amy.

Why, then, was I surprised
    at 4:30 p.m. Saturday when Derek, my oldest son, called?
He said, "They have a liver for Amy.
    We are on our way to the Hospital for Sick Children
        in Toronto."

"O ye of little faith."

As the night progresses, the magnitude of it all overwhelms us.
A five- year-old boy died of an aneurism.
Amy is now receiving his liver.

Why is so much given to us?

We have done nothing to deserve it.

At this moment Amy is still in surgery.
O my God, be with her.
Be with Deb and Derek.
Be with the Deb's parents and family.
Be with John and me and our family.
Let your name be praised.
May we all give thanks and praise you.

Derek has been calling us as they are notified
    about the progression of the surgery.
No major problems so far.
O my Lord, you are so great.
We thank you for your love and care.

Doug called for the latest report from Derek.
Doug said,
    "Amy is receiving a liver transplant
        for life and living,
    just as we receive Christ our Savior as a transplant,
        his life transplanted into ours."
Doug put it so much better than I can.

In church this morning
    the whole congregation applauded and praised God
    for the surgery that was still ongoing
    and going well.
God's people supporting God's people.

By the end of the day,
    Amy was back in her room in intensive care.
She was awake and responding
    with nods in answer to questions.

When Derek and Deb first saw her,
    they noticed the big tummy was gone!

Truly we thank you, God,
    for this miracle.
Life, your great gift, has been preserved
    in your child, Amy, this day.
Are there words to explain your greatness?
Miracles like this only say,
    "Don't underestimate the power of God."

How I love you, my God.
You are my Father!

God provides
    and we will give thanks and glorify him.
O, that he will always be glorified.

Help us not to forget your benefits, my God;
    You, my Father, are so great.

*Note: Amy was born with Glycogen Storage Disease. At five years
of age she received a liver transplant and continues to do well.*

July 30, 1988

How do you give children insight
    into being flexible in their life's choice of vocation?
I don't know.
I tried, and I know John did too.

We said,
    "God has given you the gifts to do anything you choose.
    Keep your options open and await God's call.
    Your responsibility is to respond and give him your best."

Our prayers have
    been abundantly answered.
Our four children and their partners

are all believers and active in God's work.

Thank you, Lord,
    for answered prayer.

April 23, 1989

There is a wind,
    a great wind.
The waves are powerful on Lake Superior.
Their roar is heard everywhere
    on this point of land.

God is here.
God is in the powerful waves.
God is in the wind.
God is in all creation.

O Lord, my God,
    this morning finds me alone
    but not without you.
I thought of going in to church but
    my heart,
    my soul,
    longs for quiet,
        to be in your presence,
        to feel your love fill me.

 Is it wrong to want to be
    alone with you?
Your love alone
    satisfies the need of my soul.
Your love fills me
    with renewed strength
    sufficient for many tomorrows.

"Rest in me,"
    I hear you say.
"Be still and know
    that I am God."

Sometimes I envy those
    who are now with you,
    but I know that where I am
        is where my work for you
        is to be accomplished.
To go to church today
    would be harnessing my spirit
    to man's rules of worship.

Today I need to rest in you,
    not by mankind's rules.
I need to soar with you
    as a gull soars in the wind currents,
    feeling free.

Later

O Lord, the children say,
    "Mom, I don't know how you did it
        with three children so close
        and then a fourth."
I didn't;
    you gave me the strength.
You did it.
You have always been there.
When I suffered for years
    with headaches
    people tried to tell me
        I was not right with you,
        that Satan was in me
        or in my ancestors.

O dear me!
But you were with me.
You, alone, healed me in your time
    through doctors and nurses
    and faith and love.

O Lord,
    you know what suffering is all about.
When I look at the cross
    I wonder, "How did you do it?"
What great pain:
    pain of the body,
    pain of the mind,

"For God so loved the world,
    that He gave His only begotten Son,
    that whoever believes in Him
    should not perish,
    but have eternal life,"
        you lovingly remind us in John 3:16.

I present myself to you daily.
I believe your Spirit dwells within me.
I trust that your Spirit will shine through me
    to those I meet.
I trust you, Father,
    for I am yours
    through Jesus Christ.

June 11, 1989

It is so hard for me
    to continually turn myself
    over to Jesus Christ,
        turning my all over to him
    minute by minute

emptying myself
in order to be filled
by his Holy Spirit,
giving him the reins of my life
and letting him guide me.

I keep saying to myself,
"This is ridiculous, Marney.
Take hold yourself.
You can't let Jesus do that.
You must be in control."

No!

I must not be in control of me!
Christ Jesus, my Lord, must be in control,
day and night
minute by minute.
When all is in his hands I know
true rest
and true peace.

June 14, 1989

O Lord Jesus,
I love you,
but what right do I have to love you?

You who gave up everything for all who live
or have lived in this world.
What is my love to you,
so small,
so insignificant?

And yet you say,
"I love you, Marney.

125

I will never leave you, Marney.
I will remain with you always, Marney.
I want you, Marney,
    to remain in me.
I am the vine and you, Marney,
    are one of my branches.
I will hold you, Marney,
    in the storms,
    in the breezes,
    in the heat,
    in the cold.
I will prune you, Marney.
I will feed you.
I will give you shelter.
I will be in you, Marney."

How we need to have Christ Jesus in us.
It is a completeness.
I no longer feel empty
    but filled with his love and Holy Spirit.

August 11, 1989

Lord, I give you thanks.
It is fascinating to watch
    your hand move in my life.
You lead;
    my job is to be ready
    to be filled by your Spirit.
I am your vessel of clay.

Help me to be ready
    for you at all times.
Let your Spirit dwell within me.
Let your Spirit curb me:
    curb my tongue

curb my actions
    curb my thoughts.
Let my words be your words.
Let my thoughts be your
    (more simple) thoughts.
Let me be where you would have me be.
Let me be your hands and feet.
Let me be in your will.
Keep me in your will for me.
Surround our children
    with your love and light.
Surround John and surround me.
Let your heavenly host
    surround us all.

August 17, 1989

Lord,
    these days
    you are making me aware
        of my sharp tongue
        and how it speaks
    before I even think what I am saying.
My tongue hurts people.
    Why can't I say nice things to people?
    Why can't I be more understanding?
I say unkind things.
    I belittle people.
    My face sends hurtful messages
    even before I speak!

My Lord,
    what will I do about my tongue?
Will you stop me?
You are stopping me
    by making me aware

of how I am hurting others.
Lord, I give you my tongue to control.
I cannot control it by myself.
Help me lift people up,
     not put people down.

September 18, 1989   5:30 a.m.

It is early.
The sun has not yet
     shown its rays.
The darkness is still
     surrounding us.
Even in total darkness,
     the light of God
     surrounds me.

The new day is dawning.
What will this new day bring?
What adventure will Jesus
     have for me today?
Living in the presence of God
     one never knows
     what will happen
     and the not knowing
     is exciting.

Thank you, Father.

April 9, 1990

I am having trouble with an acquaintance
     who calls herself my friend.
She takes hours of my time.
She constantly

draws attention to herself.
She tries to control me.
This morning she called,
    critical of me,
    for not doing something she wanted done.
She went on and on.
    It was intolerable.
My response was awful.
    I was anything but kind!
Lord, you know what I did.
    I hung up the phone!
Help me to ask for forgiveness.

Lord, I called Ann my spiritual sister,
    and asked her to pray for me.
What would I do without her?
You have given me
    such a beautiful friend in Ann.
Spiritually she is a great help
    and support.

June 16, 1990

I am feeling a spiritual loneliness today
    and it is no wonder.
I have not had a special time
    with you
    for a few days.
It is so very important
    for me to have this time!
My loneliness caused me to start
    looking to people.
This morning I found myself
    calling my sons, my boys,
    and that is not wrong but,
    after each call,

I felt more at a loss.
Suddenly I realized
    it is only you
    who can fill the emptiness.
Time alone with you
    and the Holy Spirit
    is my remedy for loneliness.

Lord, there have been times in my life
    when I wondered if you had left me.
That is my worst loneliness.
But, no,
    it was only when
    I needed discipline,
        and time
    to be drawn closer to you,
    to be taught dependence upon you
        alone.

September 21, 1990

It is one of my first thoughts,
    an ever present question in my mind:
    "What will people say?"

I can hear it down through
    the years of my life.
My mother often asked:
    "What will people say?"
It mattered greatly to my family.
We tried to please people
    and ended up going one direction,
    then another
    then another
    and yet another!

Who cares what people say?
They are as fickle as can be.
What I do care about
    is what does God say.

September 23, 1990

I thank God I am a woman and a wife because,
    as I learn how to abandon myself to John,
        my husband,
    I learn how to abandon myself to God,
        my Father,
    becoming completely submissive to him
        and his will for me.

The physical relationship
    between husband and wife,
    is being submissive to each other,
    not one ruling over the other
    or one being the master.
It is being completely in love with each other,
    trusting each other
    with everything and all.

As I learn to do this,
    my relationships
    with John and God
    develop to new depths.

Physically, I trust John not to hurt me
    but to let me relax
    and enjoy his love,
    as I give my body for his enjoyment
    and receive his for my pleasure.

Spiritually, it is as though I am
   married to God
   through the Son.
As I learn to relax
   and enjoy his touch,
   to be submissive to him
   and trust him,
   love and trust
   flow three ways.

July 7, 1991

My spiritual life is most important
   and then John.
Our love is a beautiful treasure
   that is enriched by God's love.
Our marriage reflects
   God's love to me.

I believe God created marriages
   to show us what our love for him can be.
To exist, both relationships must grow,
   must be given time to mature.
In both relationships
   the more time we spend together,
   the more time we want to be together.
As we become closer
   to each other,
   so we become closer to God.
The wedding day
   is just the start of growth in marriage
   as our day of salvation
   is just the start of growth in Christ.

Lord, keep me close to you.
Keep me close to John.

May the loves of my life
  be pleasing to you.

September 22, 1991   Marney's Lament
(after closing her store)

O Father,
  I am having a difficult time
  and I'm finding it hard
  and boring,
  being at home.
Doing the same thing
  over and over.
Help me, Lord,
  to see that it is worthwhile.

It is hard
  to wait for you to lead!
I do get impatient.
I want to know,
  but then if I knew what was ahead
  I would become overloaded with anxiety.

I must be patient.
I must wait patiently for you to lead me,
  doing one job at a time.
For this next week
  my calendar is full of something big
  for each day
  and that is enough.

November 13, 1991

Create in me a clean spirit.
Wash me white as snow.
Forgive my sin,
    the one I committed without thinking
    before I spoke.
I told a confidence
    about a friend
    to someone
    so she could pray with me.
Well, I found out
    I cannot do that with people.
I can never know how they will react
    or who they will tell.
In this case,
    instead of praying,
    she pointedly ignored and avoided
    the friend who needed help.
That shunning spoke
    volumes to my hurting friend.

I am really sorry, Lord.
It took a week
    for what I had done
    to sink in.
Forgive me, Lord.
Let the consequences
    of my action
    go no further.
I'm not sure
    I have really learned this lesson.
My tongue gets me
    into lots of trouble.

May 30, 1992

My thoughts and prayers are with Doug and Lorri,
    Jeremy and little Molly Rose,
    who is still in her mother's womb.
We know so much about her.
She is with us almost all the time.
We thought she was to be delivered
    into the world on May 27
    but her lungs are not where they should be
    so they will wait another week.
The doctors plan to take a needle
    to see what they find from the massive tumor, cystic hygroma,
    she has in her neck.

Medicine on one hand is so highly developed!
On the other, no cure for some diseases.

Molly Rose has so much prayer
    surrounding her,
    caring family and friends,
    love from all her extended family
    and, yet, we wonder.

We know that God can heal her
    and will heal her
    but, when,
    we do not know.

"In his time, in his time,
    he makes all things beautiful
    in his time."
        David Parkes, *In His Time*

June 11, 1992

Molly Rose has not been delivered as yet.
The tension and anxiety are with us
    but I do have a calm knowing
        that the Lord knows her
    and he is looking after it all.
He knew her
    before she was conceived.

"Come and listen,
    all you who fear God;
    let me tell you what
    he has done for me.
I cried out to him with my mouth;
    his praise was on my tongue.
If I had cherished sin in my heart,
    the Lord would not have listened;
    but God has surely listened
    and heard my voice in prayer.
Praise be to God,
    who has not rejected my prayer
    or withheld his love from me!" I sing from Psalm 66:16-20.

Perhaps this is why
    I have such peace.
I know the Lord
    has heard our prayers.
He knows what we can handle.
He knows what is best for Molly Rose
    and that Molly Rose
    will make our lives richer
    and more perfect in him.

For we, who are his children,
    are being made perfect in him
    at all times.

June 12, 1992

Molly Rose was born
    by Caesarian section this morning.
That she survived at birth
    was due to the
    God-given skills
    of pediatric and respiratory specialists.
Getting her breathing tube
    past the tumor took time and skill.
Very shortly
    she will need to have
    surgery to reduce
    the size of the tumor;
    all very risky
    but God has given us
    a miracle today.

Molly will need many more
    and for these we pray.

Note: Molly did indeed have two major surgeries to reduce the size of her tumor. After the second, her lungs failed and she was on a respirator for several weeks. She required a breathing tube placed through her neck for the next five years. Covered with prayer throughout all those years, she is now a healthy young woman. Thanks be to God!

November 8, 1992

Something that happened when my mother and dad
    took me to Alma College for Interior Design
    has flashed back into my memory.
They were so disappointed in me,
    as they often were.

I was not a good student
  and I failed Grade 10.
I had to repeat the year
  and it was a year
  of great humiliation.
Friends went on
  and I was left out.
They sent me to Alma College
  for interior design.
I never finished high school
  because I was told
  I'd never make it.
At sixteen
  I was broken.
I knew I had to stand alone
  with God.
My parents did not want me
  to disappoint my grandparents
  who were paying for my education.

Looking back on it all
  it's a wonder I didn't break up completely.
For a time,
  I was disowned.
I was a failure,
  and I felt I had lost my parents' love
Since then I've tried to earn it back
  but if feels as though I've never made it.

I am loved and always have been
  by my heavenly Father.
In my soul I know
  he has taken care of me.
He alone has loved me.
God, my Father,
  has pulled me through
  difficult days in childhood and adolescence.

There is much to be forgiven
both ways
between
parent and child.

January 3, 1993

Do we ever know ourselves?
I am constantly learning.
God is constantly moving me
this way and that way
so that I see myself
from different angles.
I need you, Lord,
to help me get off things that possess me,
off people,
even family and friends,
if they stand between you and me
and off my childish security blankets.
I need my total security
to be in you,
Jesus,
Spirit.

April 23, 1993

My worst sin is not being obedient
to God's will for me.
In order to know his will for me
I have to be in touch with him
and in order to be in touch with him
I have to be still and wait;
to be in prayer,
in conversation,
within myself.

It does not matter what anyone else
    does or thinks
    as long as God is in charge of me,
    not me
    or any other human being.
Humans love to control one another.
They want you to follow them,
    to do what they say.
It has taken me sixty-one years
    to realize this is not what God wants.
I have to be careful of this
    in all churches;
    in groups I belong to,
    groups that I identify with.
As a matter of fact,
    I can't belong to groups.
It seems John and I
    are not to belong to any church group
    until I am strong enough
    to resist being controlled by them.
We can help,
    but that is it.
This is very hard for me to understand.

June 6, 1993

I pray that our children's marriages
    will be full of love,
    husbands for wives
    wives for husbands.

I pray
    that they will have respect for each other.

140

I pray
    that our grandchildren
    will see and know
        love in their families
    so they will come to know
    and understand
        your love for them.
I pray
    that each home
    will reflect the love of Christ.

For this I thank you,
    God, my Father.

August 26, 1993

Our family cabin
    is near Fort Frances, Ontario, Canada.
In May,
    Doug's youth group,
        with several parents,
        put a new roof
        on the biggest
            and oldest cabin,
        special bonding and fellowship
        while earning funds
            toward their mission trip
            to the Dominican Republic.
This month,
    Derek's youth group
        spent a week
        putting new siding
            on the same cabin,
            the old white place,
        and one week doing
            Vacation Bible School

and door-to-door evangelism
    nearby.

All this makes an old building new:
    for retreats
    for youth missions
    for family
    for whatever.
It answers our prayer
    that God will be glorified here.

September 4, 1993

When I find myself lonely,
    down
    and depressed,
    I know instinctively
    I need to go off alone.
I need to be with God
    in prayer
    in reading of his word,
    to tell him I love him,
    that he, alone, is my delight.

O God,
    you have given me
    the beauty of your creation;
    the lake
    the woods and animals
    the rising and setting of the sun
    the moon reflecting on the water.

Such beauty
    comes from your hand.
The seasons,
    flowers and trees,

the wind,
gentle at times,
strong at times,
all of nature is beautiful,
and awesome.
But the greatest gift
you have given to me, Jesus,
is the Holy Spirit.

January 21, 1994

Following you, Lord,
day in and day out,
requires plain hard work
and a lot of plugging along!
Is that not what you do and have done
on our behalf
down through the ages?
Did Jesus not plug along,
many times alone
and misunderstood,
until finally he was scorned and crucified?
In my life,
I plugged through
discouraging times with the children
and angry times with John.
Plugging means keeping going
when I don't feel like it,
when I know it is your will
for me to keep going.

Lord, thank you that you plug along for us,
for surely many times
you have not felt like it!
Help us to keep plugging along
for your kingdom.

June 12, 1994

O Lord,
    it is such a beautiful day
    but inside,
    I cry for the sin of people.
For lying tongues and warped thoughts
    which lead to sin in all ways.
I cry for misunderstandings,
    when I assume
    people know what I am saying
    but they construe it
    to suit their own needs.

Well my Lord Jesus, you, too,
    had these problems
    and you understood their thoughts,
        their hearts,
        their souls.

People either love us or hate us.
It seems, Lord, that I do not put
    enough honey in my words.
Help me to think of the consequences
    of my words.
Help me to speak in a language
    people understand.

August 9, 1994

One of the prayers I prayed long ago
    is being answered.
I am watching a great change
    in John.
He is becoming a great leader
    in God's army.

He is my spiritual companion,
    full of God's love and compassion,
    not just for me
        but for his children
        and all those in God's kingdom.
This spiritual growth in him has come about
    as God makes a great and powerful
    move on men in this country
        using many ways,
        one of which is Promise Keepers.
God is calling men to himself
    and making men aware
    of their need for him.
The greatest gift from all this
    is that I have someone to be with me
    in the Lord.

September 5, 1994

Would I wait and watch with Jesus
    or would I fall asleep
    as the disciples did?
In my life today
    I do wait and watch with Jesus.
The waiting does get to me,
    and perhaps the watching too.
As storm clouds gather,
    as the sin in the world
    saps and sucks the life out of me,
    I stay on the alert watching with him.
Do I have oil in my lamp
    ready to move
    when I receive his signal?
Waiting, waiting, waiting,
    ready to be flexible
    to any of his commands?

It would be easy to sleep,
    to put my head in the sand
    and shut it all out!
But no,
    God help me to be
    spiritually alert with Jesus,
        waiting and watching,
            praying, praying, praying.
O Lord, my God,
    help me to stay awake spiritually.

September 20, 1994

How tender and loving is my John.
In him I see and feel the presence of God.
John has not ever put me down intentionally.
Usually it is my own misunderstanding.
He has always shown me love,
    the love of Christ
    as he has known it.
But how much more will
    the King's Son love and adore us!

I do not understand how
    he fills each of us
    with his great love,
    but he does.
He meets our every need,
    the needs we have into our very souls.

I am fortunate in having John.
He truly is a gift from God.
The Lord gave me John,
    and I can truly say that.

It was hard not having my Dad's blessing
    at the time of our marriage
    but what if I had followed his direction
    rather than my spiritual instincts?
Now at sixty-two,
    I know more about the workings
    of the Holy Spirit in my life
    (not to the fullest by any means)
    but I know the Lord's hand
    has been upon me always.

Lord God, I thank you for your gifts in my life,
    for John,
    and for your Son.
As I go forth into a new day
    I ask for your protection
    for myself
    and all whom I love and care for.

October 18, 1994

Am I self-righteous?
    I don't know.
    Maybe I come across that way!
A woman does not want me
    at the prayer group
    although I've tried
    to bend over backwards for her.
Why not?
Do I threaten her?
    What does she see?
    What does she feel about me?
Another woman avoids me, Lord.
    Is she threatened by me?
Lord, is my presence in the church
    hurtful to some?

Should I leave?
What am I doing to these women?
Questions, questions.

If I really knew myself
would *I* like or love me?
If I was looking at me from the outside
what would *I* think?
O Lord,
please help me to understand.

January 31, 1995

I expect we humans never will
know God.
I do not even know the man
I've lived with for forty-one years.
There is always something more
to learn about him.
John changes;
he grows in new ways
and so do I.

God never changes.
He is the same yesterday,
today
and forever.
He is so great.
Beyond all understanding,
he bridged the gap
by coming to earth as a baby.
He put on human form.
He lived for us,
and in his love he died
and was resurrected
for our salvation.

May 6, 1995

In my life
    if I had done better in school
    if I had not failed Grade 10
    if I had not been sent to a private women's boarding school
        to study interior design
    if I had not had one teacher who said,
        "One day you will be a great woman"
    then I would not have developed the independence
    that living away from home
    gave me.
I also might not have developed as fully
    my artistic and design capabilities.
I might not have met John,
    my husband of forty-one years.

God's will came through
    misadventure, sorrow and pain.
Certainly his will came!
The growing and learning with John,
    our beautiful growing children—
    Derek, Steve, Doug and Marney Ruth!
God in his mysterious ways has led.
But if we are his followers,
    what should we expect?

August 19, 1995

It is a strange feeling
    but a true feeling that,
    although we own our home
        and say,
    "Our home on the lake is beautiful,"
        we don't really own it or the land
        and certainly not the beauty.

We are custodians
    of the land,
    charged with making it
        more beautiful and peaceful
        for others to enjoy.
John's mother
    once said to me,
    "Plant a tree for others to enjoy,
    and it will give shade
    for many generations."
I feel that way
    about everything I do:
        the garden
        the shop
        our home
    and people enjoy
    the beauty and rest they find here.
What I really
    get pleasure from
    is sharing God's beautiful gifts with others.
My house is on loan from God.
    The lake
    the trees
    the animals
    the birds,
    belong to all God's people.
John's mother said,
    "I do not own an inch of land
    but all I see is mine."
Yes, all I see,
    all that is beautiful,
    is mine.
It is a gift from our gracious God.

July 10, 1996

Doug said
    of himself and his brothers,
    "We three have
        three different approaches
        to our Christian lives.
    We don't agree
        at all
        except in Jesus Christ."
That's amazing
    and beautiful.
Here they are,
    three grown men
    who grew up in the same home,
        under the guidance of the same parents,
        prayed for in the same way.
    Now they are three individuals
    seeing God's ways
        differently
        but all serving him.
All uniquely God's,
    praising God and
    serving his people.

July 10, 1996

How do I know
    the Holy Spirit
    is essential for Christians
    to lead a Christ-centered life?
I know because the Holy Spirit
    has revealed it
    in my own life.

Lord, I pray that your Holy Spirit

will come and continue to fill John,
giving him wisdom
and discernment in his walk.
I pray, Father, Son and Holy Spirit
that you will grow
in light and love
in each of our children:
in Derek and Deb
in Steve and Heidi
in Doug and Lorri
in Marney Ruth and Bill.
Lord, I want us all
to taste your banquet
to know your everlasting peace
to be strengthened
to grow as new creatures
through the Holy Spirit.

August 21, 1996

I am truly a pauper in my spirit.
I am poor in spirit.
When Adam and Eve
sinned in the garden of Eden,
God took away their spiritual awareness
and, as their spiritual descendants,
we are deprived.
I know the only way
to restart spiritual growth
is through Jesus.
Christ committed to me
sixty-two years ago,
but still I am a spiritual pauper.
I grow so slowly
God must be disappointed,
but he accepts me as I am.

If I turn for help to churches,
   Christian groups
   or friends,
   I am disappointed.
So my spiritual poverty
   is a matter between my God and me.

Lord, I try to grow.
I do grow slowly.
I would like to grow more deeply.

Walking Home

When the signs of age begin to mark my body
(and still more when they touch my mind),
when the ill that is to diminish me or carry me off
strikes from without or is born within me,
when the painful moment comes in which I suddenly awaken
to the fact that I am ill or growing old,
and above all
at the last moment when I am losing hold of myself
and am absolutely passive
in the hands of the great unknown forces
that have formed me,
in all those dark moments, O God,
grant that I may understand that it is you
(provided only my faith is strong enough)
who are painfully parting
the fibres of my being
in order to penetrate
to the very marrow of my substance.
and bear me away within yourself.

-Pierre Teilhard de Chardin

April 25, 1985

Today Jesus Christ is the only one
    who knows how I feel.
I feel lost.
I want to put my head down on his shoulder
    and feel his strength and calmness
    come through.

Lord, there is so much pain inside,
    a new pain I have not suffered before,
        the pain of losing earthly fathers:
        John's father and my father.

It is hard, Lord.
There is a deep groaning inside me.
    Why do they have to suffer with cancer?
    Why does it take so long for some to die?

Lord, comfort our earthly fathers
    and comfort us who sit close by
    watching their bodies deteriorate.
Give us all strength.
Give the grandchildren strength.
We, the children whose parents are dying—
    comfort and renew us.

I am so lost today, Lord.
My mind is tired;
    my strength is low.
O Lord Jesus,
    fill John and me with light and strength.
Surround us with your healing light.

July 13, 1990

I am living—right now—eternal life!
Life that will never end for my spirit.
My body will die
    but not my spirit,
    nor anyone's spirit
        who has come to you
        through the Son.
We have eternal life!

I wish I had, earlier in life,
    looked upon living
    as I do now.
Each day is a new mile for you, Lord,
    in my spiritual journey.
It truly is a walk through
    a foreign land.

But, God, I am looking forward,
    even yearning,
    to *go home*
    to eternal life in heaven with you.
I am instinctively unafraid.
I am instinctively led
    to push on with life.
Keep me open to your Spirit.
May someone each day
    see you through me
    that they, too,
    may enter your eternal life.

November 6, 1991

Lord, when my body fails me,
    when it is my time to leave
        to come to you,
    please let your light flow in
        and around me.

Let your holy presence be glorified.
May I glorify you at all times
    but especially,
    in the death of my body.
Please radiate through it.

November 15, 1992

As I get older
    I pray that my armor
        will get stronger;
    that I will be used
        by God often;
    that my strength will be in him;
    that my eyes will be on him;
    that my spirit will be filled by his Spirit.

I do look forward
    to being with him
    when it is time.

At my funeral
    I don't want a eulogy.
I just want people
    to know
    who I follow.

April 8, 1994

Lord, this morning John and I were talking
    about what will happen
    when one of us
    goes first to be with you.
It is not dying that is hard.
It is my being left without John
    or John being left without me.
It will be very difficult.
There will be pain of a kind
    unknown to us now.
I don't look forward to this certainty.
Neither does John.

O Father,
    you alone know how
    we will manage.
You alone will comfort us.
But Lord,
    even with my hand joined with John's,
    and both our hands in yours,
    growing older
    is lonesome and scary.

September 6, 1996

As you know, Lord,
    on this body I live in,
    cancer has shown up, a malignant melanoma.

I am in a bit of shock.
Lord, I don't know what to pray
    except please fill me with
    your holy presence
    so I will be filled with your glory.

I know I will have
    all the human responses to this cancer
    but please help me
        to accept it
    and do what is wise
        for your glory,
    so that others may see you
        reflected in my life.

Help me to be strong,
    and if my body
    is to die with this cancer,
help me to die
    in your glory
so that good may come from it
    and many people
    will see you
        through me.

You, my Lord,
    have given me everlasting life
    through your Son, Jesus Christ.
I will not die.
I will live forever
    with you.
I will not die.
You will come
    to deliver me.
Not only that
    but at the right time
    you will come
to deliver my husband, John,
    and, much later, my children,
    to be with me
and I with them and you.

September 10, 1996

Tomorrow I have surgery.
Friends and loved ones have supported me,
    phoned me,
    are close.
Doug is coming up to be with John and me.
The Lord is close.
He is right here
    and we travel together.
Tonight I don't have any feelings
    except his love surrounding me.

"Make every effort to live in peace
    with all people and to be holy,"
        Paul says.
"Without holiness
    no one will see the Lord.
See to it that no one misses
    the grace of God
    and that no bitter root
    grows up to cause trouble
    and defile many,"
        (Hebrews 12:14-15)
    and so I pray.

Father, there is a boulder
    in the path of my life,
    a malignant cancerous growth.
It may all be cut out tomorrow
    or the doctors may not get it all.
Whatever happens, Lord,
    I pray that you will
    be glorified
        and many will
        see your grace.

September 13, 1996

Lord, I am recovering
    from my surgery
    two days ago.
I am waiting for the
    pathology microscopic report.
I am not afraid
    nor am I anxious.
I am interested in knowing
    but no matter what,
    my God is with me.
The 23rd Psalm
    keeps me going.
"The Lord is my Shepherd,
    I shall not be in want.
He makes me lie down in green pastures,
    he leads me beside quiet waters,
    he restores my soul.
He guides me in paths of righteousness
    for his name's sake.
Even though I walk
    through the valley of the shadow of death,
I will fear no evil,
    for you are with me;
    your rod and your staff,
    they comfort me.
You prepare a table before me
    in the presence of my enemies.
You anoint my head with oil;
    my cup overflows.
Surely goodness and love will follow me
    all the days of my life,
    and I will dwell in the house of the Lord
    forever."

Later

Psalm 16 is my psalm
    for today.

"Keep me safe, O God,
    for in you I take refuge.
I said to the Lord,
     'You are my Lord;
    apart from you I have no good thing.'
As for the saints who are in the land,
    they are the glorious ones
    in whom is all my delight.
The sorrows of those will increase
    who run after other gods.
I will not pour out their libations of blood
    or take up their names on my lips.
Lord, you have assigned me my
    portion and my cup;
    you have made my lot secure.
The boundary lines have fallen for me
    in pleasant places;
    surely I have a delightful inheritance.

"I will praise the Lord, who counsels me;
    even at night my heart instructs me.
I have set the Lord always before me.
Because he is at my right hand,
    I will not be shaken.
Therefore my heart is glad and my tongue rejoices;
    my body also will rest secure,
    because you will not abandon me to the grave,
    nor will you let your Holy One see decay.
You have made known to me the path of life;
    you will fill me with joy in your presence,
    with eternal pleasures at your right hand."

September 15, 1996

The report is back.
I will need major surgery
    with lymph nodes removed.
I doubt I will be able
    to sit for weeks!
Today, although I am usually
    strengthened by God's love
        and by John's love,
    I am feeling a void,
        an emptiness,
    a horrible feeling
        of lostness.
Lord, forgive my weak faith.
Strengthen me
    through your Holy Spirit.

September 21, 1996

Home from the hospital.
I am hurting
    but it is a *healing* pain.
"Therefore we do not lose heart.
Though outwardly
    we are wasting away,
    yet inwardly
    we are being renewed
    day by day.
So we fix our eyes
    not on what is seen,
    but on what is unseen.
For what is seen is temporary,
    but what is unseen is eternal,"
        I remember Paul saying in 2 Corinthians 4:16, 18.

I cannot focus my eyes
    to read or write any more.
Lord, I am yours.

September 24, 1996

The past weekend
    was, as the kids call it,
    a real "bummer."
Tears and more tears,
    pain and drain
    but God never leaves me.
Friends call or come
    with cards
    flowers
    prayers.

"May the God of hope fill you
    with all joy and peace
    as you trust in him,
    so that you may
    overflow with hope
    by the power
    of the Holy Spirit,"
        Paul says in Romans 15:13.

That is what I hope:
    that God's Holy Spirit
    will fill my weakness
    with his strength
and help my body
    and spirit
    to soar as if
        on eagle's wings.

Later

As I look out of my window,
    as I lie in bed,
    the lake is so blue,
        the sun so warm,
        the sky so clear.
I rejoice in the God
    of all creation.
The flowers
    are pushing out
    their last blooms
        and the colors
        are vivid!
The cool nights
    and warm days
    seem to intensify
    their beauty.
Isn't God's way beautiful?

I hope I am like the flowers.
In my last days
    I want to show my most brilliant
    colors for him!

Later

I've not been perfect.
I have big cracks
    in my vessel.
I've not been kind
    at times.
I've certainly not been
    what people wanted
    me to be.

But I have tried to be
    what my heavenly Father
    intended me to be
    living in his will,
    and reflecting his love.
He has been
    so good to me.
So I keep my eyes on Jesus,
    God in human form,
    and my pain dissolves
    as I look upon his face.

Later

O Father,
    I weep with sadness
    and with joy.
I want to be with you
    but I don't want to
    leave my John
    and I don't want
        to leave my children.
Lord, can't you take us
    all together?
O Lord, I can't stop crying
    for my heart breaks for John.
He has been your
    right hand man
    for me here on earth.
He has taught me,
    he has loved me
    no matter what.
He has supported me
    even when I was
    unkind to him.
O Lord, I love him.

Can't you take us together?
Lord, we are like Canada geese,
    paired forever.
You gave us to
    each other.
We have loved
    since we first touched.
We both knew
    we were for each other.
Comfort him, Lord,
    and bring us soon
    together again
    in your arms.

September 29, 1996

"Come and follow me,"
    our Lord asks us.
Am I following him?
Am I keeping my eyes
    on the cross
    as I endure the pain?
If I did take my eyes
    from Jesus and the cross,
    I doubt I could
        endure the physical pain
        of my body.
Lord, what pain Christ
    endured for me!
The physical pain of the crucifixion
    must have been terrible.
The spiritual pain
    worse.
Thank you, Jesus.

The surgery is still painful
    but God's Holy Spirit
        has filled me
        with tools to cope with it.
He prepared me
    in the healing
    of my headaches.

October 5, 1996

Now comes the fight
    to repair and overcome
    the damage of cancer.
Pick up the pieces
    so to speak
    and on with life,
        a different life
        with a swollen leg
            that doesn't always do
            what I want it to do,
With a body that is not perfect,
    with parts missing.

I am brought back
    to the army hospital in Okinawa
    and a soldier with stumps
    for legs and half an arm blown off.
He returned to his family
    and has done amazingly well.
This is what I must do too.
God will not let me
    lie around
    feeling sorry for myself.
With your help, Lord,
    I can do all things
    because you strengthen me.

October 9, 1996

A card came with this poem:

> What Cancer Cannot Do
>
> Cancer is so limited...
> It cannot cripple love
> It cannot shatter hope
> It cannot corrode faith
> It cannot destroy peace
> It cannot kill friendship
> It cannot suppress memories
> It cannot silence courage
> It cannot invade the soul
> It cannot steal eternal life
> It cannot conquer the Spirit.
> *Author Unknown*

This is true
    but I cannot help wondering
    how much more of my body
        will be reduced by cancer?
    Is it eating
        at another unseen part of my body?
        Will my swollen leg
            go down?

There are so many questions,
    but I cannot know the answers now.
Wouldn't it be fine to be able to go to a doctor
    and ask him those questions
    and have him know the answers?

Only God knows the answers.

171

October 23, 1996

Life is strangely beautiful
    even in suffering
        be it cancer,
        heart problems,
        or whatever.
When we look up to
    the cross, to the crucifixion
    of Jesus, of God,
We see that Christ knew
    why he came.
He knew the outcome
    yet he lived
    each moment
        for his Father,
        for the glory of God
        and for God's will.
I know why I am here.
We all know the outcome
    of life on earth
    will be physical death.
I know, Lord,
    that your gift
    of faith to me
        means my spirit
        will live forever.
Forever with you Father,
    with your Son,
    and with your Holy Spirit.
Beautiful, isn't it?

November 5, 1996

Lord, I am completely
    without thought this morning.
I need you to fill me.
Where is your Holy Spirit?
I want to feel
    the comfort of your presence
    with me, right now!
I want to lean back
    and feel the comfort
    of your protecting wings.
I am tired
    and since the surgery.
I am unable to
    get
    with
    it.

November 13, 1996

Lord, my God, creator of all,
    it is almost two months
    since my horrible cancer surgery.
Lord, my God,
    I want to weep and weep–
    not on the outside,
    but inside I cry.
O God, I hurt.
I can't get my energy up.
I wake each morning
    hoping for that energy
    to be back
        but it isn't yet.
Lord, my hope
    is built in you.

My God, rest my mind;
    relieve it of useless worry.
Lord, send your Holy Spirit
    to calm and guide
    my way.

November 14, 1996

Steadily yesterday
    I seemed to pick up more energy.
I was able to see a pattern of living
    I can tolerate:
    rest in the morning
    work in the afternoon.
You truly do send your Holy Spirit to me!

November 29, 1996

It has been difficult
    to write in my journal
    since the surgery.
I am able to pray
    but there are times,
    like now,
    when I feel far from God.
I know he is beside me
    though.
I think now
    my life will be more praying
    than writing.

December 18, 1996

I may be a frozen Cornish hen
    (so to speak)
    with missing parts.
I may have cancer pouring from my pores.
I may be physically falling apart
    but I am alive forevermore
    through the finished work of Jesus Christ.
Because he has overcome I, too,
    am able to overcome the world.
His Holy Spirit is alive within me.

January 15, 1997

It is in knowing
    that God has given me life eternal
    through his hand
    in his very own Son, Jesus Christ.
It is in knowing
    that his Holy Spirit lives within me,
that I do not have to do anything
    but live peacefully where I am
    in whatever situation I am in.

This morning I have been
    in an agitated way.
There is so much nothingness to do.
My leg is giving me problems and pain.
I have to go to a new massage therapist today.
I am in a state of push and agitation.

I need to stop and say,
    O God, I love you.
You have given me eternity to get things done.
Please, let your Holy Spirit quiet me down.

Give me peace and love
    so your love will flow through me.
Please let my visit with the new therapist
    be a good experience.
Help me to relax in you,
Let me have your peace.

January 25, 1997

The last few days
    I've been interested in a change in me.
I've been brought up
    to be critical of those who call themselves Christians.
I've been brought up
    to be critical of those who differ
    from people of other denominations.
"They couldn't be *of Jesus*!"
They were wrong!

Now I'm asking,
    "Isn't it wonderful what the Lord is doing
        through this or that person?"
I'm searching for
    a reflection of Jesus in people.
In some there is an abundance,
    in others a fleeting glance,
    but what *a game*
    to try to find Jesus in others!

No, I don't have the only way
    but this one thing I know:
    My relationship with him
        is personal.
It's a growing relationship,
    and he puts my roots down in him.

Like Paul I must be alone with the Holy Spirit.
It does not matter what people think
    (even other Christians).
I need to be *free in the spirit of God,*
    going by the Holy Spirit's
    direction for my life.
In order to do this
    I must be alone with his Holy Spirit,
        with the triune God,
            seeking his will for me.
I, like Paul after his conversion, need to be alone
    with the Holy Spirit and with Jesus.
I must learn to be intimate
    with God, the Father,
    God, the Son, and
    God, the Holy Spirit.

January 31, 1997

I have been so tangled up
    with the complexities of church.
I find John so almost naively simple
    in his faith.
His bringing up,
his Christian heritage,
    does not bind him to follow
        the do's and don'ts of other Christians
    but simply to live for God
        as he is led.

Evangelicals can become very bogged down
    in their own dogmas.
All denominations can.
I must not get bogged down again
    but keep my eyes on Jesus.
Paul says to keep our eyes on the goal.

The goal is not a specific denomination
    bogged down with its own
    interpretations and doctrines.
No, that's not "where it's at."

God wants each of us today
    to fill the corner where we are,
    to lighten it with his love.

February 24, 1997

As I sit here
    praying and being in fellowship
    with God,
    I realize I love these times alone
        in his presence.

At times, I also feel
    the presence of my family
    who have gone before me.
It seems as though
    their love,
    their holy love,
    surrounds me.

I am at the stage now,
    with this illness,
    of just letting go,
    not pushing against it,
    but letting God use me
    where I am.

I am resting in his arms.
O how thankful I am
    that I am in the palm of his hand.

February 26, 1997

Lord,
    my strength and my energy
    seem to be zapped.
I know I am to be happy,
    to be full of your light and love
    even though I am zapped.
"Godliness with contentment is great gain.
For we brought nothing into the world,
    and we can take nothing out of it.
But if we have food and clothing,
    we will be content with that,"
        Paul says in 1 Timothy 6:6-8.

Help me to be content, Lord.

March 5, 1997

We are at the Buena Vista condo in Puerto Vaillarta.
Our friends have just left.
Their oceanside condo had no reservations for them
    so we invited them here.
Looking at the spiritual side of this,
    we have friends for life and eternity
    in Donna and Joe.

It really amazes me,
    (I wish I could put into words),
    my feelings—my utter amazement
    as to how many Christian
    brothers and sisters we have!

We don't have to judge
    whether or not they are children
    of the kingdom

179

or if they are *so-called* saved.
We need to be open
    to seeing God's Holy Spirit in them.
If there is a mustard seed of faith,
    (and usually there is that and more)
    then that is sufficient.
My camping mentor was right when she said forty years ago,
    "Marney, when you look for what you agree on
        and not what you disagree about,
        you will find a lot more Christians in the world."

God's rule is
    the cross and
    the resurrection.
That is all.

April 4, 1997

It is so hard to write.
I struggle and struggle.
It seems my strength
    just isn't there.

April 9, 1997

I would like to have new parts for my body
    to replace those which surgery has taken away.
It matters deeply that the surgeon had to
    cut away parts of me.
I will never be the same again;
    my libido is gone
    my femininity is deeply bruised
    my eyes are full of tears.

O Lord, I hurt,
    not just physically
    but spiritually
    to my very core.
I will never be the same again.
(The phone keeps ringing,
    and I keep sitting.
It is better than having to talk.)

Maybe death is better than "surgical life,"
    but
    there are so many kinds of pain
    and my pain is not great in comparison.

I wonder if there had been no surgery
    and I had died,
    would it have been better?
Either way there is great loss.
Part of me now is gone forever,
    and I mourn that loss.
Today I feel it greatly.
I can only share my pain in writing.
There seems to be no comfort
    from this pain.
Just a lonely, lost feeling
    that does not go away.

Later

It is so hard to be interested in others.
I would like to be shut out
    from everyone.
Yes, I'd like to die.

It would be nice if Jesus would come.
It's a wonderful thought

but, until then, death is more a reality.

Lord, help me
    not to let others
    see my discouragement.
Help me
    to find things I enjoy doing,
    things I can do.
Right now I don't want
    to be with people.
I don't want to talk.

I want to rest and heal.

I love you, Lord.
I love living in your presence
    even if I feel these things.

Later

Surgery may cure,
    but what pain!
Cancer surgery is different
    from any other surgery I have had.
A radical vulvectomy is—
    so physically and spiritually
    crippling and disabling.
It has robbed me of vitality.
It seems to penetrate right to my soul.
It has robbed me of my femininity.
I feel so much older.
The excitement of life is gone.
My nights are full of dreams
    where my whole life,
    all mixed up,
    passes before me.

My mind seems to be trying
    to sort itself out.
It is all so confusing!
The things I must accomplish in a day
    (which are limited)
      I have to force myself to do.
I cannot sit in a straight chair;
    it hurts too much.
The shop looms so,
    over my head.
Will I ever get back to normal?

But I must, like the Psalmist,
    "be at rest in the Lord."
Be at peace with him.
I must rest in his arms.

Later

There is a pair of robins
    who have been in the yard now
    for two days.
I do hope they will stay.
It is cold out,
    but they sing.
It warms my heart.
How horrible it would be
    without the song of birds
    —even the song of gulls
    as they call out to approaching spring.
Sadie, our dog, has wandered in
    and is sitting by my chair.

How I would like to curl up
    in the arms of God
    and rest...and heal.

Later

"Be at rest once more, O my soul,
    for the Lord has been good to you.

"For you, O Lord, have delivered my soul from death,
    my eyes from tears,
    my feet from stumbling,
    that I may walk before the Lord
    in the land of the living,"
        the Psalmist continues in Psalm 116:7-9.

I am sure this illness
    affects each person differently and
    I wonder if our wealth of knowledge
        does not give us more
        physical
        mental
        spiritual
        pain.
The rush of life that we have
    imposed on ourselves
    which our grandparents did not know;
    what is it doing to us?

Later

Yesterday I was feeling so down
    with my progress.
It is very hard to continually
    have to push myself.

"I love the Lord, for he heard my voice;
    he heard my cry for mercy.
Because he turned his ear to me,
    I will call on him as long as I live.

"The cords of death entangled me,
    the anguish of the grave came upon me;
I was overcome by trouble and sorrow.
Then I called on the name of the Lord:
    'O Lord, save me!'

"The Lord is gracious and righteous;
    our God is full of compassion.
The Lord protects the simplehearted;
    when I was in great need, he saved me.

"Be at rest once more, O my soul,
    for the Lord has been good to you,"
      Psalm 116:1-7 says.

I need to rest in the Lord
    and how good the Lord has been to me!

Lord, I am like the Psalmist today.
I wonder why this had to happen.
One moment I was fine
    and the next day, surgery.
Now, six months later,
    I am slowly, very slowly, recovering.

It is so hard to keep going;
    I have to push myself.
I get so exhausted—
    but I can pray.

April 10, 1997

My soul longs for the Lord, my God.
How I adore you,
    my God,
    the lover of my soul.

185

I will arise and shine
    for I am full of his light.

As the water outside my window
    sparkles like diamonds
    as it reflects the rays of the sun,
    just so I will sparkle in the reflection of his light.

This morning there is a choir singing,
    a choir of robins' voices,
    with the sweet trill of song sparrows,
        chickadees and finches.
A flicker is outside on the lawn
    digging for grubs.

Lord, how often I think of your children
    all over the world
        singing in choirs,
        but especially the ones who dig for grubs,
        the ones in prison for their faith
        or in countries torn apart by war
        or struggling against death because they love you.
Lord, bless and be with them all,
    for only you know who they are.

Later

Encircle John in your light and love
    as he ministers to his patients.
He retires in December.
For him it is unknown territory
    to be without work or a paycheck.
Lord, give him peace
    —your peace.
Give him security
    —your security.

Give him wisdom
　　—your wisdom.
Help him find your will for his
　　and our lives.

Later

You, my Lord,
　　have given each of your children
　　a task throughout life on earth;
　　to find your will,
　　a never ending mystery,
　　　　a real hunt!

As I face a new day, I wonder:
　　What will today bring?
　　Will I handle it well?
　　Will I bring glory to you?
　　Where will I find you today?
　　Will I see a new direction?

I love you Lord, my God.
I love the Lord,
　　for he has heard my voice.
He has heard my cry for mercy.
I will call on the Lord as long as I live.
He hears my cries of pain.
He hears my cries of joy.
He brings me songs of joy
　　in the singing of birds.
He fills my home
　　with their choir of song.
His Son warms the rooms of my soul.
His angels watch over us.
I am filled with his strength and power
　　even though I am weak.

His gifts are many.
I will delight myself in him always.

How great thou art,
    my king of kings.
How wondrous are your ways.

May 4, 1997

The days since I last wrote
    have been long and hard.
I had vaginal surgery
    and, suddenly,
    one week later,
        I had severe pelvic pressure and pain
            and hemorrhaged.
I was taken to St. Luke's hospital
    for further repair to stop the bleeding.
After six pints of transfused blood,
    I'm tired and exhausted,
    but not like before.
My bottom is sore!

Many thoughts, many prayers,
    by many people
    have gone up to my heavenly Father.
His holy presence is always within me.

Having to slow down and let others help me,
    makes me think and remember
    how we need each other
    to help us through life.
It does not matter about wealth or status.
What really matters
    is our love for one another
    and the Lord.

May 19, 1997

This morning, Lord, I feel lost,
    very lost.
Perhaps I have a bad attitude about everything:
    the store,
    both stores,
    gifts and food!
Lord, I feel so alone,
    so alone,
    even though I am surrounded by people
    each going their own way.
Lord, I feel even you are distant today.

I need your Holy Spirit
    to fill me with life anew.
This illness and its complications
    have left me at a low ebb.

Please, Lord,
    "Create in me a pure heart, O God,
    and renew a steadfast spirit within me.
    Do not cast me from your presence
        or take your Holy Spirit from me." (Psalm 51:10-11)
Forgive me my sin.
Lord, fill me with your spirit.

Romans 8:35, 38-39, is a good reading
    for me this morning.
"Who shall separate us from the love of Christ?
Shall trouble or hardship
    or persecution or famine
    or nakedness or danger or sword?
For I am convinced that neither death nor life,
    neither angels nor demons,
    neither the present nor the future,
    nor any powers,

neither height nor depth,
    nor anything else in all creation,
will be able to separate us
    from the love of God that is in
    Christ Jesus our Lord."

June 3, 1997

God is an intimate God.
    He knows every detail of our lives.
    He knows I am sorting things out.
Things like:
    How am I to handle this large leg?
    What must I do to overcome
        the *down stage* I am going through?

I always need to remember
    the closeness of God,
    the triune God, to me.
He surrounds me with his love.
Psalm 25:12 promises that he will instruct me
    in the way I am to go.

Lean not on your own understanding
    but on every word from the Lord.
Wait on him in silence.
Listen for his voice.
Know that he loves you and
    is molding you in his image.

As I learn to live
    in the presence of God
    I won't even know
        that I am in his presence.
It is as natural
    as breathing in and out.

August 4, 1997

The choice I have made
    is to worship the Lord, my God,
    as Jesus has shown me.
To follow his way even unto death.

I have to be so careful
    that I am not controlled by people
    but by God, the Father;
    God, the Son,
    and God, the Holy Spirit.

Father God, Jesus Christ,
    fill me anew with your Holy Spirit.
Let the light of your love and peace
    shine through me always.

August 7, 1997

To live in oneness with
    the triune God,
to be filled with the living Christ,
    moment by moment,
to know that I walk through each day,
    as one with God,
these are my goals.

John and I are one,
    but I do not know where or what
    he is doing when we are apart.
Being one with God
    through his Son, Jesus Christ, though,
    means I am never separated or alone.
Even in death he will be with me.
His rod and staff will comfort me.

September 21, 1997

I've come from the shop
    with a funny kind of pain.
My legs are tired and painful
    and I am exhausted.
I've decided to take a bath.

While in the bath
    God says,
    "I am in the waters
        of Lake Superior.
    You, my child,
        have always loved large lakes.
    You have found me in Lake Ontario,
        Lake Erie,
        Georgian Bay,
        in the oceans.

    "I am the force of the waves
        and the gentle breeze of calm days.
    I am in the birds
        and the flowers of your garden.
    Look at the lilies of your garden,
        what majesty they are clothed in,
        what color schemes.

    "You are my child.
        You don't need to worry about attending church.
        You have learned all they can teach you.
    Now come and learn with me.
        Let me lead you.
        Soar with me.

    "There is a special part of me
        that is completely yours.

You do not understand this but
    I am so vast that for each person
    there is a part of me.
For each person that ever lived
    or is living or will be,
    there is enough of me
    to live within each one.

"You cannot put me in a box.
The children of Israel tried that, but
    do you think I stayed within the ark?
It was only a symbol of me.

"No one can confine me or my Spirit
    or call me *theirs*.
People have tried but my Spirit always leaves.

"I am in each person who comes to me
    childlike in spirit and in truth.

"I am simple, so simple
    that many people of intellect
    cannot easily find me
    unless their faith is childlike and pure.

"As I walk and talk with you,
    as I communicate with you,
    you hear my quiet voice in stillness.

"You have heard me for many years.
You have listened to my voice.
You have gone my way.
Shun leaders who would distract you.

"I will lead you.
Follow me.
I am leading you."

September 24, 1997

Today I have been wondering
    about the changes in our lives:
        John's retirement
        my having cancer.
There are a lot of changes!
I cannot do what I used to do.
I tire quickly.
But I believe God is with us
    and he does not expect us to keep
    the pace we had
    at forty to fifty years of age.

We will never know what we have done for God
    or how we have been used by the Spirit.
There have been works of God
    exhibited through us.
People have been blessed.
Most often we don't know about it.
But God does.

I wonder what God has for us now.

July 8, 1998

Today I have received
    many cards
    messages of prayer
    beautiful Scriptures.
I know many brothers and
        sisters in Christ
    are praying for me
but those cards
    are not comforting today.

I have a quietness.
I have a peace.
The person who brings
    great calm to me
    is John.
His steady love
    and care mean the most.
What a gift that God
    has given me in John,
        my earthly lover.
But together
    we are one in Jesus Christ
    forevermore.

July 15, 1998

Lord, I hurt.
    Help me to live with this pain,
        a pain that engulfs me at times.
    It's too early in the progress
        of this tumor – or perhaps it isn't!
    Help me to live
        in your glory.
    Help me to live
        in your will.
    Help me to die in body
        giving you honor and praise.
You, Lord Jesus,
    conquered death for me
    so that my soul
        will not die.
    I will live eternally
        with you.
Now I am going through
    the metamorphosis
    into your holy light.

July 19, 1998

If within his world
    God allows people
    to die from cancer,
what right have I to complain?
Yes, I cry.
Yes, I want more time with my family,
    more time with John.
Time is ever more precious
    as the cancer grows.
I don't want to die yet,
    but in my deepest being
        I accept the cancer
        and anticipate the joy
            of going to be with God.

A lot has happened to me
    in my lifetime.
I've tried to follow God's plan
    and God's will for me,
and I'm not finished yet.
    Perhaps I won't be finished
    until eternity itself is "finished."

I felt I heard the Lord
    talking to me about Jesus' death
    and his suffering,
    telling me to accept my own.
I am unable to put into words
    what I think I heard
but I know my triune God
    is with me
and I know he will
    become stronger
    as I grow weaker.

I pray.
I know that through Jesus Christ
    I will have peace.
    His Holy Spirit surrounds
        and strengthens me.
    I will not be alone.
God will send his angels now
    and later,
        to carry me to God.

July 19, 1998

In my physical pain and
    my physical suffering
I must remember
    that Paul tells us
        suffering leads to perseverance
        perseverance to character
        character to hope
    and hope does not disappoint
        because it is God's hope
        poured out into our hearts
            by the Holy Spirit.
    How fortunate I am
        to be living
        covered by Jesus' sacrifice
            for the atonement of my sins.
I live under the certainty
    of bodily death.
I live under the certainty
    of spiritual immortality.
Sometimes I feel
    I want to leap from this body.
    I want to fly
    I want to sing
    I want to laugh with the joy of the Lord

I want to heap praise onto him
but, alas, I cannot do this
    the way I am
        (except in my soul!)
    for my left leg
        gets in the way.

No earthly human being
    can give me the comfort
    that my triune God does.
There is no alternative
    to the hope I have
    in Jesus Christ.
He goes before me.
He breaks the barriers
    of death.
He suffered for me
    for my sins.
He is with me
    all the time
    forever.
Jesus Christ is my treasure.

July 20, 1998

The gulls are so busy
    feeding their young
    on our Lake Superior island.
        So much noise they make,
        the mothers oblivious to all
            except feeding their young.
    If their squealing was not there
        I would miss it.
The quacking mallards
    are there too.

The song of the sparrow
    adds to the melody.
The cawing of the ravens
    gives another dimension
    to the bird chorus –
beautiful gifts from God.

I was picking a few flowers
    for the table this morning
As I was walking to shut
    off the garden hose
    with a small bouquet in my hand
    a hummingbird came
        to the flowers
        spending a moment close to my hand.
That hummingbird reminds me,
    as God's creation often does,
    that he is with me,
    that this small
        little
        delicate bird
    has the same Creator I do
    and that God cares for sparrows,
        hummingbirds
        and me.
To be ill at this time
    is not too hard,
    for God's nature
        keeps me company.

I do see God.

July 25, 1998

I am selfish.
I want people to admire me.
I want to look like a holy person,
      like a martyr.
I ask, "Lord, how do you see me?"
    and he answers,
"You are a small goat
    wanting to get your own way,
    butting at me,
    balking at my way for you.
Your patience is short.
You try to fix things Marney's way,
    not waiting for me to act.
You forget that
    I am always with you.
You know it,
    but you won't experience it.
Then, on your own,
    trouble comes
    tragedy strikes.
Take me off the shelf
    and bring me back
    to guide your life
    again."

September 4, 1998

As I near the "finish line"
    in this body
I feel more and more
    that I am to glorify him.

Whoever comes to visit me
  will know
  that I belong to Jesus
  for he has redeemed me by
        and through the cross.

When Jesus was in the Garden of Gethsemane
  Luke says,
  "An angel from heaven
      appeared to him
      and strengthened him."

God continues to send
  his angels
  to strengthen me.

Printed in the United States
44315LVS00005BA/157-258